Cambridge Elements ≡

Elements in Histories of Emotions and the Senses
edited by
Rob Boddice
Tampere University
Piroska Nagy
Université du Québec à Montréal (UQAM)
Mark Smith
University of South Carolina

MARKETING VIOLENCE

The Affective Economy of Violent Imageries in the Dutch Republic

Frans-Willem Korsten
Leiden University

Inger Leemans
Vrije Universiteit Amsterdam

Cornelis van der Haven
Ghent University

Karel Vanhaesebrouck
Université libre de Bruxelles

CAMBRIDGE
UNIVERSITY PRESS

Shaftesbury Road, Cambridge CB2 8EA, United Kingdom

One Liberty Plaza, 20th Floor, New York, NY 10006, USA

477 Williamstown Road, Port Melbourne, VIC 3207, Australia

314–321, 3rd Floor, Plot 3, Splendor Forum, Jasola District Centre, New Delhi – 110025, India

103 Penang Road, #05–06/07, Visioncrest Commercial, Singapore 238467

Cambridge University Press is part of Cambridge University Press & Assessment, a department of the University of Cambridge.

We share the University's mission to contribute to society through the pursuit of education, learning and research at the highest international levels of excellence.

www.cambridge.org
Information on this title: www.cambridge.org/9781009246460

DOI: 10.1017/9781009246446

When citing this work, please include a reference to the DOI 10.1017/9781009246446

First published 2023

A catalogue record for this publication is available from the British Library.

ISBN 978-1-009-24646-0 Paperback
ISSN 2632-1068 (online)
ISSN 2632-105X (print)

Marketing Violence

The Affective Economy of Violent Imageries in the Dutch Republic

Elements in Histories of Emotions and the Senses

DOI: 10.1017/9781009246446
First published online: August 2023

Frans-Willem Korsten
Leiden University

Inger Leemans
Vrije Universiteit Amsterdam

Cornelis van der Haven
Ghent University

Karel Vanhaesebrouck
Université libre de Bruxelles

Author for correspondence: Inger Leemans, i.b.leemans@vu.nl

Abstract: This Element describes the development of an affective economy of violence in the early modern Dutch Republic through the circulation of images. The Element outlines that while violence became more controlled in the course of the seventeenth century, with fewer public executions for instance, the realm of cultural representation was filled with violent imagery: from prints, atlases and paintings, through theatres and public spectacles, to peep boxes. It shows how emotions were evoked, exploited and controlled in this affective economy of violence based on desires, interests and exploitation. This title is also available as Open Access on Cambridge Core.

This Element also has a video abstract: http://www.cambridge.org/korsten

Keywords: affective economy, violence, early modern history, market, cultural techniques

ISBNs: 9781009246460 (PB), 9781009246446 (OC)
ISSNs: 2632-1068 (online), 2632-105X (print)

Contents

Introduction: The Affective Economy of Violence   1

1 Engineering Images: Commercial Remediations
of Violence   12

2 Desire: From Theatrical Accumulation
to Deep Spectacle   25

3 Interest: Collective Self-Interest Construed
and Contested   40

4 Control: Unruly Power, Civilising Markets   56

5 Exploitation: The Affects of Empire   71

Conclusion: The Violence of Markets   87

References   90

Introduction: The Affective Economy of Violence
Violence Sells

The world, as presented in Romeyn de Hooghe's engraving *Spaanse wreedheden in West-Indië* (*Spanish Tyranny in the West Indies*) (Figure 1), is an extremely violent place. This early modern print draws the viewer into a grim explosion of violent scenes crammed into one complex image of Spanish conduct in the colonies. Attracting Western readers to the 'exotic' world of the West Indies, with palm trees, tree huts and volcanoes, the artist confronts the viewer with a series of examples of violence. These range from the military attacks of Alvarado and his conquistadors in Brazil, and their destruction of Indigenous buildings, via the brutal slaughtering of the women and children, thrown into a pit filled with spikes, to the 'burning and boiling' of chiefs and the feeding of their bodies to the dogs and birds. The cruelty and disrespect for the human body are not limited to the Spanish conquerors: the West Indian cannibals are likewise abusing human bodies. Essentially, the image suggests that violence is not only a fundamental aspect of human behaviour but an altogether natural phenomenon. Volcanic eruptions, fires and floods violate human civilisation, but human existence is also analogous to these phenomena. The dramatic, dynamic narrative of this detailed, high-quality engraving by the hand of the skilled artist Romeyn de Hooghe thus imagines the human, animal and natural world as a most violent place.

De Hooghe presented this elaborate engraving in a beautiful oblong book of around fifty folio prints, printed with care in c.1700 by the famous Leiden publisher Peter van der Aa, entitled *Les Indes Orientales et Occidentales, et autres lieux* [...] (*The West and East Indies and Other Places Represented in Very Beautiful Pictures*). For this catalogue of his artistic mastery, de Hooghe re-edited various engravings he had produced decades earlier for the *Curious Remarks about the Most Remarkable Matters of the East and West Indies*, a multivolume ethnographic study by Simon de Vries (1682). Extracting his engravings from this previous study, in *Les Indes Orientales et Occidentales* de Hooghe presented images without the interference of long pieces of text. The addition of bilingual (French/Dutch) colophons helped the viewer understand what they were looking at, without the need to really take their eyes off the image. De Hooghe thus turned the reader into a spectator.

From this one depiction of Spanish tyranny, the viewer could move on to new scenes of violence: the cruel punishments of the Asian magistrates, the uncivilised medical 'cures' of Indian doctors, the dehumanising slave trade of the Turks, the slaughter of children in Abyssinia, human sacrifice in Mexico, the pain of poverty, the rape of women, the deafening sound of fireworks, the

Figure 1 Romeyn de Hooghe, *Spaanse wreedheden in West-Indië*, in *Les Indes Orientales et Occidentales, et autres lieux* [. . .]. (Leiden: Pieter van der Aa, c.1700). Rijksmuseum Amsterdam, BI-1972-1043-40.

relentless force of natural disasters and the grotesque, devouring monsters of the Asian and African animal kingdoms (Figure 2).

Moving from image to image, the viewer could experience different emotions: shock, awe, anger, disgust, curiosity or pleasure. Our contention in what follows is, however, that this abundance of images *engineered* an *affective economy* in which violence played a dominant role, as it affectively bound people to not just one world but a multiplicity of worlds. In this context, prints can be analysed as affective commercial products that had a deep impact on the emotional practices and self-fashioning of early modern consumer audiences.

The prints showed all types of violence, from legitimate to illegitimate, from cruelly human to natural, from European to exotic. De Hooghe's workshop alone produced more than 3,500 prints, of which an amazingly large proportion are extremely violent in nature (Nierop, 2018), ranging from relatively small and detailed depictions to gigantic violent scenes. Print woodcuts, engravings and etchings for illustrated books, broadsheets, pamphlets and atlases were central to one of the key market spaces that provided the Dutch Republic and a much wider audience with an explosion of violent imagery. While Dutch paintings presented more peaceful scenes – landscapes, city scenes, still lifes, interiors, portraits – an impressive proportion of the Dutch print market

Figure 2 Romeyn de Hooghe, *Aziatische en Afrikaanse dieren*, in *Les Indes Orientales et Occidentales, et autres lieux* [. . .]. (Leiden: Pieter van der Aa, 1702). Rijksmuseum Amsterdam, BI-1972-1043-11.

concerned the visual staging of violence (Duijnen, 2019). Engravers and printing houses produced new modes of imagining atrocities, with depictions of public executions, sea battles, tales of martyrs, torture handbooks, battlefield scenes, horrifying Old Testament stories, exotic tyrannical 'justice', beheadings, rape, pillage, iconoclasm, furies, raids, shootings, stabbings, piracy, looting – in short, nearly every form of violence imaginable (Duijnen, 2018). Apparently, books like these were not meant to rationally reflect on the role and functions of different kinds of violence. Rather, all kinds of violence were brought together as a matter of fascination. Violence became a product that sold. Consequently, whereas in what follows different forms of violence will be addressed, we consider violence in the same way as it was sold: in all its variants.

The affective commercial product of *Les Indes Orientales et Occidentales* was carefully crafted and put into a narrative by de Hooghe and his publisher, Pieter van der Aa, both famous and skilled entrepreneurs at the peak of their careers (Hoftijzer, 1999; Nierop, 2018). Both were deeply invested in bringing images of violence to the book market (Gottfried, 1698). However, the impact of this violent imagery by far exceeded the intentions of their makers. The images had already travelled a long way – not only from the book of Simon de

Vries to this book of prints but also from other print collections. De Hooghe's print shop eagerly copied representations of the practices, rituals and riches of the world from older images and illustrated books (Schmidt, 2015). De Hooghe's engravings became iconic themselves, informing other prints, frontispieces and broadsheets. His ethnographic prints, for instance, found their way into another impressive image enterprise: the *Galerie agréable du monde.* In this series of sixty-six volumes, Pieter van der Aa compiled around 3,000 plates from famous Dutch engravers for the 'lovers' – 'liefhebbers': amateurs – of history and geography (1725; cf. Peat, 2020). This collected graphic knowledge of the world and imaginative enterprise highlights the explosion of printed images which had started to flow into the European market over the course of the seventeenth century.

Capitalist Market and Affective Economy

De Hooghe's case allows us to highlight two domains that will be of relevance throughout this Element: markets and affective economies. Dealing with the market of imaginations of violence, we will consider (calculable) material conditions of production, transport, trade, exploitation and consumption. Representations of violence can be compared to commodities such as sugar – one of the new products from the Americas that became a dominant mass commodity in Europe and which involved a new industry and system of production and trade (Abbott, 2010).

In the concept of *affective economy* two terms come together that for a long time were studied separately: affect and economy. While economics and economic history traditionally disregarded emotions and embodiment (or talked about them to highlight how they interfered with rational economic processes), the more recent field of the history of emotions initially displayed little interest in matters of commerce (for introductions to the history of emotions, see Reddy, 2001; Frevert, 2011; Plamper, 2015; Broomhall, 2016; Boddice, 2017). Historians of emotions hardly paid any attention to economic factors or to commercial actors using, influencing or producing emotions (Bailey, 2017).

Recent trends, however, show more interest in the intersections between emotions and economies. Studies describe the role of emotions in the origins of capitalism, the psychology of market behaviour and the cultural values, imaginations and moral issues which influence market behaviour (Schleifer, 2000; McCloskey, 2006, 2016; Goldgar 2008; Yazdipour, 2011; Fontaine, 2014; Margócsy, 2014; Leemans & Goldgar, 2020). Sociology and cultural philosophy studies analyse emotional labour and the marketing of private life (Hochschild, 1983; Illouz, 2007). In political theory, emotions are studied for their cognitive potential and their potential to create or split social bonds within political systems (Nussbaum, 2013). If, in this context, we say the Dutch Republic witnessed the emergence of a capitalist market, this was, obviously, not the industrialised version of the nineteenth century. The Republic's version of capitalism is characterised by the cycle of production and consumption and the materialisation of a mass market. The immense production of images did not answer to the demand from a mass audience; it called on that demand and made the mass audience possible. This form of capitalism did not serve the individual needs of consumers; it bound them to a market, which is precisely why recent studies have put forward the concepts of 'emotional economies' and 'affective economies' (Ahmed, 2004a; Leemans & Goldgar, 2020).

The cultural theorist Sara Ahmed employs the concept of affective economies as an analytical tool to understand the workings of collective identities. Although she uses the words 'emotion' and 'affect' sometimes interchangeably, the term 'affect' seems more apt, as it underlines the fact that emotions do not work just on an individual level but are mediating, communicative tools, connected to expressions of feelings, which help to shape society. A 'theory of emotion as economy' may show that emotions work as a form of capital: 'affect [. . .] is produced only as an effect of its circulation' (Ahmed, 2004b: 120). The role of the media was crucial in this context because they defined 'how bodies and ideas become aligned with each other' (Lehman et al., 2019).

These recent studies interpret affective economies, however, mostly on an abstract level. Economic terms such as production, exchange and accumulation are mainly used metaphorically, describing psychological 'emotional households' and 'moral economies' balancing different emotions and accumulation value in terms of human capital (Frevert, 2011). We would rather steer the concept towards economics and sociology, where it is used to understand the workings of modern-day consumer societies and the emotional investment that capitalist societies require from their participants (Casey & Taylor, 2015). If violence, as an issue of emotional investment, became a marketed product, how did creative producers tap into the affective imagination of projected consumers to 'invent' and stimulate their desires for horror and adventure? Can we map the emotional-commercial components of the affective market of imaginations of violence?

By choosing to work with the concept of 'affective economies' rather than 'emotional economies', we aim to highlight that we are interested not (only) in individual desires and responses but also in the *embodiment* (the sensorial aspects) and in the *social* and *spatial* aspects of commercial processes (Trigg, 2016). The term 'affect' allows us to analyse, firstly, how image markets put the *mind, the body and its sensations* into different states. Watching violent scenes may cause the body to tremble with anxiety, shake with disgust or seriously lose control – for instance, by causing nausea. Accordingly, as early modern artists displayed bodily sensations through various media, they mediated affective relations that went beyond the confines of a 'dialogue'. Producers and consumers together explored the body language of violence and the embodied sensations that violent imagery could bring.

Secondly, affect underlines the *social, communicative, binding and splitting* aspects of emotions (cf. Broomhall, 2016; Boddice, 2017). Emotions can act as *emotives*: they communicate, investigate and connect (Reddy, 2001). Once expressed, an emotion requests a response. 'emotions *do things*, they align individuals with communities — or bodily space with social space — through the very intensity of their attachments' (Ahmed, 2004b: 119). Thus, emotions can be at the basis of *interest*, in that they bring people into interrelation. Shared feelings can be a strong basis for shaping communities, just as they can split communities. The emotional communities of image markets are, as we will show, *bound by interest* – by the self-interest of the satisfaction of desires but also by the invested interest of shared experiences (see Section 3). Thirdly, and finally, affects are embodied, at work *between* bodies, and *enacted* through different media, in spaces such as theatres and anatomical theatres, in maps, on frontispieces, in public manifestations such as firework displays and so forth.

The Affective Economy of Images

The map in Figure 3, from around 1647, shows Pernambuco, a region in northern Brazil which at the time was controlled by the Dutch West India Company. The map was created as part of a series of fifty-five maps and accounts of the travels of Count John Maurice of Nassau to Brazil in the years 1636–44. In terms of representation, it is hard to speak of one image. Rather, it is a set of different kinds of images with some explanatory text. To a general audience of consumers, the horrors connected with sugar production were consciously concealed to avoid spoiling the desires and pleasures connected with sugar. In the upper, empty part of the map, almost as a symbol of the idea of *terra nullius* that would legitimate colonial appropriation, a sugarcane mill is represented, with people working peacefully, and, in the left-hand corner, a social community is eating and playing.

Economically and ecologically speaking, sugar production involved a set of new lifeworlds, which took the shape of a plantation culture that affected all actors deeply and was not restricted to the Americas (Abbott, 2010). Seventeenth-century Amsterdam, for instance, witnessed the growth of more than 100 sugar refineries that redefined urban space, changed technologies, attracted people and

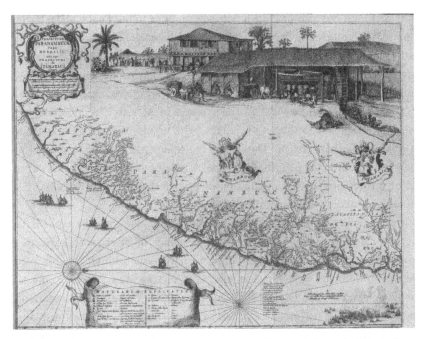

Figure 3 Salomon Savery, *Map of the Coast of Pernambuco* (1645–7), in Caspar Barlaeus, *Rerum per octennium in Brasilia* (Amsterdam: Johannes Willemsz Blaeu, 1647). Rijksmuseum Amsterdam, BI-1972-1043-11.

came with their own affective economy (Poelwijk, 2003). The sugar industry produced new 'bodies of interest': connecting sweet-addicted consumers with the blood and sweat of the (enslaved) labourers in the Netherlands and overseas. The production, distribution and consumption of sugar were in turn connected to the production of a wide variety of (decorated) sugar pots and other imaginative sales products, with their own affective forces of appeal. The violence needed to produce sugar was conspicuously absent from such luxury commodities, which serves to show that affective economies can work with asymmetrical distributions. However, for some observers – Europeans who had helped to construct and oversee the plantations or former slaves and other black immigrants – the violence behind the seemingly peaceful scene might have been more visible or even painfully embodied. The working of affective economies depends on the perspectives of the participants.

In the case of the map of Pernambuco, violence is explicitly presented in a low-key manner in the lower right-hand corner, where a sea battle is depicted between Dutch and Spanish-Portuguese fleets close to the island of Itamaraca in January 1640. The battle was part of an expedition led by John Maurice (see Section 5) that would not only lead to the WIC's conquering parts of Brazil but also provide a decisive impulse to the Dutch slave trade. Though the violence is explicitly thematised here, the aim and goal of the battle remain implicit again, or are a matter of epistemic violence, as when the territory of Indigenous people is suddenly captured by projections that follow the logic of compass roses, producing a map that represents northern Brazil as owned by European powers. In the context of affective economies, one question, then, is how the set of images, with a map of the region, a scene of a sea battle between the Dutch and the Spaniards and the depiction of a sugar plant, affected people at the time. Another question is how this entire set of images propelled a circulation of affects that was intrinsically connected to a much wider field of imageries.

If violence in itself became something that sells, or that was to be avoided for the sake of selling things, this was both a matter of markets and affective economies. Violent prints, like the ones we have dealt with so far, informed and were informed by paintings, maps, plays, coins and even luxury objects, such as porcelain cups (Jörg, 1997; Dijkstra, 2021). The prints also stood in dialogue with live performances, such as public festivals, firework displays, lotteries, fairs or public executions. That is, violent images circulated among a large variety of sectors, causing a situation where viewers could be confronted with, or would be seduced to seek, particular kinds of imagery again and again, imprinting the mind and body with certain forms, typologies and knowledges concerning violence. The circulating images were a matter of what we called, in a previously published article, '*imagineering*' – on which more in Section 1.

Aim of This Element

One may ask, obviously, whether the market for, and marketing of, violent imagery was a new phenomenon. Have not humans been confronted with violent images for centuries? We contend that a fundamental shift took place in the early modern period, with the emergence of modern, capitalist economies, the commodification of images and the expansion and interconnection of different image industries and markets. These developments not only led to an explosion of images; they also caused shifts in the affective impact of images, on the individual level and on the level of societies at large. This shift merits scholarly attention, not least since it represents an essential stage in the development of our modern-day visually oriented societies.

In this Element, we aim to showcase what happened in the seventeenth century when images started to circulate widely as marketed products, in and between various sectors of society, connected with staged scenes and visual materials and driven by commercial impulses and marketing strategies.

The staple market of images was analogous, here, to the staple market of all goods – or entrepôt market – as the cornerstone of the fast-expanding and globalising Dutch economy (Wallerstein, [1980] 2011: 56). The more the Republic and its hub Amsterdam got involved in a wider European network of trade first and then a global one, the more voluminous and diverse this storage market became (Vries & Woude, 1997). The profitable bulk trades in grain and fish were followed by less bulky but very profitable 'rich trades', with spices and silk as paradigms. The Dutch East India Company (VOC) was a massive supplier in this context and sent 4,700 ships out to Asia between 1595 and 1795, with close to a million people involved (Lucassen, 2004). This staple market depended on high-volume storage (bulk), technologies (bigger ships that could be built more quickly, at lower cost and equipped by a smaller crew), information exchange, trading agents and means of distribution (Lesger, 2006; Zanden, 2009).

Similar factors propelled the 'staple markets of images'. Our question is what it did to people. What affective economy did these image markets develop? What media technologies and social techniques were used by producers to create desires, attracting readers and spectators and keeping them interested? Why did people invest in visual products and productions? How did images engineer specific impacts and mobilise embodied reactions? What profit or interest did they bring? We will show how images engineered not only individual responses but also collective forms of behaviour and how images tried to control the affects they aroused.

In the early modern period, the development of the print industry, the advancement of the art market and the market for luxury goods, as well as the commercialisation of other cultural sectors, such as theatres, resulted in the production of a swirl of images (Haven et al., 2021). One dominant body of images was extremely violent in nature. As we will argue, it was through and in connection with this 'spectacle of violence' that new ways of looking and embodied experiences were introduced. As the public manifestation of violence by ruling powers became less dominant, violence could become a matter of private yet mass consumption as a commodity to be enjoyed. Readers could become addicted to scenes of horror and war or consume images to help understand humankind's violent nature. Affective communities could develop around the collective consumption of violent images, rendering specific affective practices.

Marketing Violence will give the modern-day reader a sense of the wide spectrum of the early modern representation of violence by discussing various types of violence in a variety of cultural sectors, ranging from gigantic paintings of sea battles to bloody plays, peepshows presenting battlefields, anatomical

Figure 4 Abramah Magyrus, *De wonderlijke historie der mensche-eeters, verhandelende haren aart, oude woonplaatsen* (Amsterdam: Jan ten Hoorn, 1696). Rijksmuseum Amsterdam, RP-P-OB-44.578.

atlases, prints of public beheadings, poems, maps and ethnographic prints of cruel customs – such as the frontispiece of *The Marvelous History of Cannibals* (1696) (Figure 4). This frontispiece is an example of remediation: different media are translated into one another. It is first of all a book's frontispiece, with the publishing house named below. Secondly, the print is a visual equivalent of what will be described *in* the book. Thirdly, the cloth above suggests that the curtain has been raised to reveal a theatrical scene. Working together, the imagery brings violent histories to life. In this Element, we aim to analyse what kinds of violent images the different sectors of the early modern cultural market produced, explain how these different sectors intersected and show how images were constantly remediated.

Our underlying thesis is that the seventeenth-century shift towards a commercial market of the imagination helped develop a new affective economy. We chose to analyse this phenomenon in the Dutch Republic as a paradigmatic case. The early modern Northern Netherlands offers an excellent example of both an economy that was capable of producing and consuming violent imageries and an affective economy of violent imagery. It was one of the first states to develop into a modern, capitalist economy, with a cultural market that served as a *magazin de l'univers* that produced and distributed maps, illustrated books, paintings, luxury objects and other imagery throughout European markets and beyond (Vries & Woude, 1997; Israel, 1998; Zanden, 2009).

Although we see violence as just one possible example of the development of an affective economy based on the commercial production of imageries, we will also argue that the imagination of violence played an essential role in the forging of the Dutch Republic and its imperial, colonial programme. The stunning abundance of violent imagery that inundated Dutch markets in the course of the seventeenth century can be interpreted as an instrument of mediation between (1) the urgent commemoration of the violent past from which the Republic had matured; (2) the decline of explicit scenes of violence in the public sphere in most of the provinces; and (3) the advancement of an ideal of a moderate, peaceful, tolerant, commercial Republic that was at the same time (4) a military power at the centre of a new commercial empire.

Sections

Section 1 introduces the reader to the early modern staple market of images and will present the market strategies, media technologies and the social and affective techniques of early modern image production and consumption. Section 2 analyses desire as a driving force in the affective economy. The section focusses on a fundamental transformation in the early modern world from theatrical regimes closely coordinated by sovereign powers into a culture of spectacle, driven by commercial market mechanisms. Desire, in this context, is considered as a common affective drive that can be propelled and used by market actors. Section 3 follows this line of investigation but now with *interest* as a pivotal term. The section asks why people became so invested in scenes of violence. What interest was involved for producers, consumers and sociopolitical parties? Here, we investigate fireworks, peepshows, battlefield scenes, public uprisings and their remediation. Starting from personal profit-seeking and self-interest, we will discuss interest as an embodied force and as a social drive, which operate in gift economies and webs of investment.

Section 4 wonders how the affects were controlled. The issue is both how people were controlled by violence and how the vehement affects aroused by scenes of violence could be made productive. We will discuss different agents of enactment and control of violence, ranging from the markets in general to specific stock markets, or from stadtholders to burgomasters, and all somehow connected to a powerful and familiar source of both excessive violence and control: divine violence. The underlying thesis is that both governmental and civil market control came to be more and more connected to people's self-control, which implied controlling the passions. Among other media, the section investigates cartoons and poems. Section 5 brings us back to the question as to why the Dutch Republic was so involved in depicting and staging violence. Through a discussion of atlases, illustrated ethnographies, architectural façades, depictions of sea battles and scenes of slavery, we will show the inherent tension underlying the Dutch political and imperial project. On the one hand, it flaunted its strength and colonial might through visual power plays, while, on the other hand, it tried to avoid explicit references to violence inflicted on humans and nature or tried to push this to the margins. Exploitation thus incorporated the interplay between pride and unease.

Finally, we present a conclusion on what we call 'the affective loop'. Desires, anxieties, fears and hopes drove markets, just as much as these emotions and affects were driven by the market. Here, we propose an integrated approach to affects and emotions, not isolating them to the domain of the psyche, the body, the private, the collective or any one of the domains of life. As the seventeenth-century Dutch marketing of violence shows, affects run throughout, or connect, the whole gambit of societies and lifeworlds.

1 Engineering Images: Commercial Remediations of Violence

Selling Violence: An Entrepôt of Images

The production of images, whether in visual or rhetorical imaginations, provided the Amsterdam entrepôt market of goods with an equivalent in a staple market of images, with traders getting them in, producing them, storing them, selling them and distributing them in relation to the demands of the market and the day (Montias, 2002; Marchi & Miegroet, 2006). Over the course of the seventeenth century, the Dutch Republic developed into a cultural hub for the Republic of Letters and established itself as *le magazin de l'univers* – 'the bookshop of the world'. It is estimated that Dutch printing houses published more than 350,000 editions (Pettegree & Der Weduwen, 2018).

The Dutch knowledge economy, perceived as the first knowledge economy of Europe, filled the European book market with printed texts, propelled by an advanced creative industry of printers, artists, engravers and map-makers (Zanden, 2009; Kolfin & Veen, 2011; Haks, 2013; Rasterhoff, 2017). During the seventeenth century, the Calvinist-dominated Republic slackened its religious hesitance towards images. It is estimated that a total of no fewer than 5 million paintings were produced in the Golden Age Dutch Republic. Most Dutch households had paintings or other kinds of imagery hanging on their walls (Montias, 1982; Bok, 1994; Loughman & Montias, 2000). The Dutch book market embraced the visual, printing illustrated Bibles and providing all kinds of illustrated books to an apparently profitable market (Stronks, 2011). Images were everywhere.

These images – prints but also architecture and decorations – proudly presented the Dutch Republic's powerful place in the world (Bussels, Eck & Oostveldt, 2021; Schama, 1988; Israel, 1998; Prak, 2005). One telling example is the majestical Amsterdam Maritime Warehouse of the Admiralty, built in 1655–6. The visual theme of the façades of this building, attributed to Artus Quellinus, is Janus-faced. One tympanum entitled 'Zeevaart' (shipping) is oriented towards the sea, and the tympanum 'Zeebewind' (sea rule) is oriented towards land (Figure 5).

'Zeevaart' shows an allegorical representation of Holland's maritime endeavour. A water nymph, the symbol of the city of Amsterdam, begs Neptune to bring her the treasures of the sea – and they are brought, almost naturally, although all packaged. Here, the representation of violence is absent. 'Zeebewind', however, expresses the ruling authority of the Admiralty, symbolised by a woman wearing a crown of ships and standing on a shell that is safely anchored while being served by sailors who carry a flag, a sword, a cannon, a gun carriage and gunpowder. The two frontispieces taken together were an explicit illustration of how a commercial centre, the hub of an impressive fleet of commercial ships that sailed the seven seas, was at the same time a centre of military power. The Republic had a fleet, consisting of different building blocks but united under one flag and capable of defending itself and the commercial bodies under its protection. It was also eager to attack others to open up new markets. The tympana thus proudly present a net of commerce and violent power.

Poets such as Antonides van der Goes and Joost van den Vondel explained how the Maritime Warehouse and its frontispieces should be read. Their texts added new images to what the frontispieces already showed. Vondel's eulogy, for instance, depicts the function of Dutch maritime power as follows:

> It pleases me to see the foam rush down its sides
> To hear how it snorts when fleets of war arrive
> Victorious from the sea, hauling banners with them

(a)

(b)

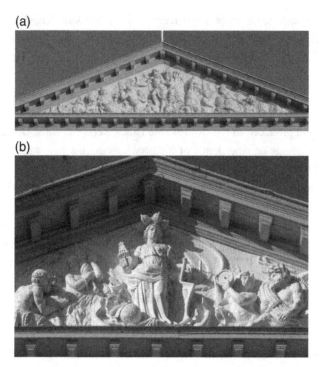

Figure 5 Tympanums of the Amsterdam Maritime Warehouse: (a) 'Zeevaart' oriented towards the sea; (b) 'Zeebewind' oriented towards land. Pictures: Klaas Schoof. Amsterdam – Architectuur in beeld.

> And flags, charged by the plundering of enemies.
> Nature and necessity teach everyone to wake up in danger
> To arm one's self, and to preserve oneself against violence
> To put into practice what divine providence granted him
> As a weapon against disaster and lamentation. This issue
> Is safeguarded by everything that lives, whether it has reason,
> Or a sensitive life, or is just capable of growth.
> Thus, the tree arms itself and its fruit with foliage and bark
> And cortex and peel, against cold and heat and cold.
> Thus, God arms the snake with scale and sharp tongues
> And deadly poison; thus, the lion throws its whelps
> In a hiding place and cavern, in fear of loss.
> Thus, he is equipped with sharp claws and teeth.
>
> (Vondel 1935: 655, lines 21–35)

As can be seen, image is added upon image in a logically arranged association of forms of violence connoting defence and attack that ground the Republic's use of violence in the law of nature. Nature is there from the start, with the foam of the sea. Yet the foam shifts into foam caused by a fleet of warships that comes rushing in, carrying the spoils of war. To play down the possible aggression inherent in this image, Vondel immediately adds that violence is natural when caused by the Dutch *nood*: 'need', 'distress', 'want' and 'necessity'. To safeguard beings against need, divine providence has equipped all natural beings, including all flora, with forms of protection. Such forms of protection easily become forms of attack, when necessary. A snake can use its deadly poison, and a lion will first protect its cubs by hiding them but will use its deadly claws and formidable teeth when pushed.

The image of the lion is a dominant one: the lion was the symbol of the province of Holland and in general for the new Dutch Republic (Figure 6). As this image makes clear, the lion was partly a symbol that could ground the use of violence in natural law. At the same time, the sword carried by this lion and its inscription 'Patriae dei' indicate that the newly installed Republic had divine support and was well equipped with instruments of war.

Although the rise of a vibrant visual culture in the Dutch Republic has been studied previously, few studies have examined the imagery of violence separately, and few studies have researched the technologies employed across

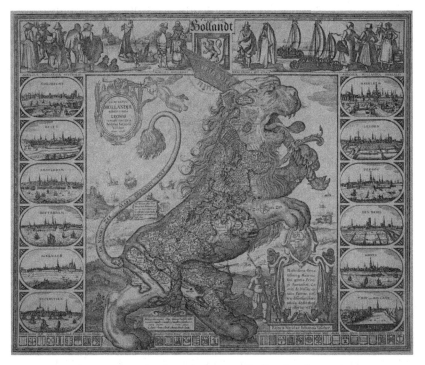

Figure 6 Claes Jansz. Visscher, *Comitatus Hollandiæ denuo forma Leonis* (1648). University Library Amsterdam, HB-KZL I 1 A 1 (10).

different media with the aim of understanding the affective impact of these webs of images on early modern audiences. Two characteristics of the new cultural industries and markets were their capacity to innovate technologically and to *remediate* the material at hand, constantly renewing topics, themes and motives by rearranging them, redesigning them, translating them to other media or bringing them up to date according to new quality standards (Davids, 2008). One theme that is especially apt to illustrate this was the recycling of the visual representation of so-called *tyrannieën*, or furies, such as the Spanish fury – whether in the Southern Netherlands or in the Americas – the Turkish fury or the French fury (followed in the eighteenth century by the English fury). These furies formed a counterpoint to the image of the noble but forceful lion in that they could not be captured metaphorically by one image but instead by a multiplicity of images.

Images, Media and Remediation: Recycling Furies

In 1672, the Republic experienced a decisive moment in its history when England and France shortly after one another (and in close consultation) declared war. Whereas the war with the English was mainly a matter of sea battles, German and French troops almost effortlessly invaded the provinces – though in the course of no more than a year the Dutch water defences exhausted them and they were forced to retreat (Hale, 2007; Reinders, 2010; Prud'homme van Reine, 2013). In several instances, atrocities occurred that were instantly thematised and marketed. For instance, the atelier of Romeyn de Hooghe started to put out broadsheets which covered the news events in changing combinations of scaffold scenes, crowd action, *tableaux vivants*, portraits and texts. Figure 7 shows two such prints, which were part of a series entitled *French Tyranny in Dutch Villages*. The scenes present a catalogue of atrocities inflicted on Dutch men, women, children and livestock, and on their lifeless bodies, as part of the devastation of wealth and property. The images are constructed in such a way that the viewer's eyes cannot rest but are drawn from horror to horror.

Not only did de Hooghe 'staple' violent images within one broadsheet, in the context of the series of cruelties, almost all his prints were also copied frantically, transformed and reprinted. This was often done anonymously by publishers profiting from the fame of the master of violent images but also by famous artists such as Jan Luyken and Bernard Picart. These violent scenes remained popular, moreover, until the end of the eighteenth century. People could buy the series of prints, separate scenes taken from them or other combinations with or without textual explanations.

(a)

(b)

Figure 7 Romeyn de Hooghe, (a) *French Tyranny in a Dutch Village* (1672). Rijksmuseum Amsterdam, RP-P-OB-77.197; (b) *French Tyranny in a Dutch Village* (1672). Rijksmuseum Amsterdam, RP-P-OB-77.199.

While being innovative both technologically and artistically, these prints by de Hooghe were the product of a longer tradition of prints depicting cruelty which were entangled with the coming of age of the young Dutch Republic. For instance, in 1633 a set of eighteen etchings was published under the title

Les grandes misères et malheurs de la guerre, or *The Great Miseries and Misfortunes of War* (Figure 8). This work by Jacques Callot is commonly considered a first powerful statement in the history of European art against the atrocities of war, comparable to Goya's pieces on the issue in the early nineteenth century. Callot's images started to travel through Europe in different versions. One set was republished in Amsterdam somewhere between 1677 and 1690 under the title *The Sad Miseries of War: Very Nicely and Craftily Depicted by Jacques Callot* (Schenk, 1670–90).

The considerable number of studies of these etchings pay almost no attention to the differing status and power of the printing press between 1633 and 1690 (Goldfarb, 1990). Yet, although the set published at the end of the century was the same as the one from 1633, it was defined by a radically different cultural and political infrastructure, with different affective implications. The more general problems of atrocities of war had become more specific because the Republic had been invaded by French forces. As a consequence, Callot's etchings were taken up intertextually in new sets of images, such as de Hooghe's depictions of the *French Tyranny in Dutch Villages* (1672), thus recycling the theme of furies.

Growing out of the revolt against Spanish rule, the Republic had put violent prints to good use, enticing anger about Spanish 'tyranny' and its cruel furies, creating support and enthusiasm for the revolt and, later on, imprinting these historical atrocities on the minds of later generations (Baudartius, 1610). The continuity and shifts in the tradition of atrocity propaganda in Dutch popular print and the repetitive character of scenes of atrocities have been described and catalogued (Cilleßen, 2006; Duijnen, 2020). From the St Bartholomew's Day Massacre, via the Spanish tyranny and the 'black legend', to the French fury, we find comparable depictions of plundering, stabbing, shooting, the slaughter of

Figure 8 Jacques Callot, *Les grandes misères et malheurs de la guerre* (1633).
Rijksmuseum Amsterdam, RP-P-OB-20.656.

women and children in the marketplace, rape, the cutting up of female bodies, hanging, men being thrown out of windows, burning, ransacking houses, destroying property and the piling up of bodies. The function of these images resided partly in their informative quality, distributing news about the war. They had persuasive influence – for instance, to keep the provinces involved in military campaigns. And they could function as instruments for memorialisation politics, as when they had a role in the development of a national myth in which the free and tolerant Calvinist Dutch Republic was counterpoised against 'black legend' Catholic Spain (Nierop, 2009; Pollmann, 2017; Kuijpers, 2018).

On a more general level, the images also appear to have explored violence as a concept, presenting inventories of cruelty and analysing violence as a cultural phenomenon. In the second half of the seventeenth century the violent narratives became more intimate and personal, shifting away from scenes of mass executions, bird's-eye views and cartoon-style pamphlets with multiple scenes towards depictions of more isolated moments of violence, zooming in on the affects aroused in the participants (Duijnen, 2019). Such images were produced by, and for, a *market*. Both the repetition of and the variation between images indicate an advanced cultural market, where any possible saturation of the market was met with diversification. By the middle of the seventeenth century, the Dutch book-and-print market seems to have reached its peak in terms of producers and production, offering cultural products and luxury goods that were almost endlessly varied (Rasterhoff, 2017). We can analyse this in terms of 'familiar surprises': products that combine familiarity and comfort with novelty and thrill, and can therefore both cater to known publics as well as specify new target groups (Hutter, 2011: 204; Rasterhoff & Beelen, 2020). Repetition and variation thus sustained the image market.

The repetition and variation were often also a matter of *remediation*. Remediation takes place when images are taken up, or repeated, through other media, with each new medium incorporating contents and forms of previous media (Bolter & Grusin, 2000). For instance, prints in books often followed a theatrical logic in how the scene was represented. Callot's scene presented in Figure 8 followed the characteristics of a *tableau vivant*, as it was staged in theatres. Images from one medium could be translated to another medium, then. For instance, when in 1672 the republican leaders of the Republic, the De Witt brothers, were slaughtered, their capture, killing and lynching were depicted through prints and paintings. The prints travelled through different media, including books, booklets and broadsheets. Coins, yet another medium, were minted following a design based on the printed images, while other coins later appeared in print. Repetition and remediation led to a multitude of visual and textual stagings of the event, allowing the public to relive and absorb it from every possible angle and perspective by reading about, watching and, in the case of coins, touching it. Such remediation could facilitate so-called hypermediacy – that is, a reflective awareness of the medium or media used (Bolter & Grusin, 2000: 11–14). For instance, the Callot print's use of a theatrical frame may have led the audience to reflect on the image as if staged and theatrical.

The seventeenth century witnessed the development of an extensive, trans-national, commercial and representational infrastructure of images in different media. This infrastructure involved technologies that, although developed for one medium, could easily be adopted by others, such as when paintings were turned into engravings, prints formed the basis of *tableaux vivants* or the logic of the theatre was transformed into portable miniature theatres by travelling showmen. This led to different balances between forms of immediacy and hypermediacy. How did this material and representational infrastructure of images come to affectively redefine the way in which subjects understood and felt themselves to be actors in the world?

Constructing Selves and the Articulation of the Real

All the diverse technologies of representation that shaped consumers' affective intertwinement with images were connected to specific agents: printers, engravers, machine builders, shop owners, consumers. Yet their actions taken together were a matter of what we called elsewhere *imagineering* – a present participle that is a contraction of imagining and engineering (Haven et al., 2021). In the first instance, the term 'imagineering' was coined in the domains of urban studies and the creative industries, albeit with different meanings. The origin of the term can be traced back to an advertisement from 1942 by Alcoa, The Aluminum Company of America, in *Time Magazine*, which states: 'Imagineering is letting your imagination soar, and then engineering it down to earth' (Sailer, 1957; see also Suitner, 2015). In this context, *imaging* came to be defined as a strategic use of images to represent urban environments, whereas *imagineering* indicated a process in urban development 'where discursive meaning-making functions as a legitimation and stabilization of certain material practices in planning' (Suitner, 2015: 98). In other words, in the fields of urban studies, theme parks and game design, the term refers to the translation of imaginary representations of an environment into material reality.

Yet another form of imagineering is at work when people talk about 'Disney imagineers' (Best, 2010: 196). The latter term was not chosen at random: the research and development branch of the Walt Disney Company, which designs and creates its theme parks and attractions, is called 'Imagineering', which is why Disney has trademarked the use of the term – which is also why the publisher asked us not to use the term in the title of this Element and as a main concept. In relation to Disney, one definition of imagineering was: 'The conscious creation of places with characteristics similar to other places (as in Disneyland). Often seen as the creation of a superficial veneer or façade of culture' (Knox & Pinch, 2010: 328). The terms used in this quote, 'superficial' and 'veneer', suggest that imagineering is considered the postmodern counterpart, here, of the lucidity, or the materially 'real stuff', of modernist architecture.

Central to our study is a baroque kind of image production. In the context of the early modern entrepôt market of images, the material production of images constituted collective forms of imagination that worked as a cultural technique producing distinct historical selves. This is not only a matter of engineering imaginations into materiality (prints, paintings, plays, staged spectacles); it is also a powerful cultural technique that defines how people find themselves affectively embodied in the world. The aspects of this cultural technique are:

- a set of *formal technologies*, such as those of painting, etching and printing or making theatre, spectacular shows and so on that allow for different forms of mediation and remediation;
- a set of *market strategies*, which allow for a complex interaction between producers, consumers, cultural agents and media; and
- both *individually* customised and *collective techniques*, aimed at serving but also construing individual and collective selves. That is, readers or viewers were taking in circulating images that, in turn, had an influence on how they found themselves in the world.

Just as the early modern commercial market in goods was possible only due to new technologies – for instance, in shipbuilding and wind-driven woodcutting – the market for images depended on technological and aesthetic innovations. If Dutch printers produced more extensive and expensive atlases, for instance, these were based on new technologies in printing, cartography, engraving, binding and so forth. Likewise, the realisation of the first Amsterdam theatre concerned not just the construction of a building but a building that facilitated new technologies of representation. In turn, these functioned as cultural techniques producing historical selves (Bruyn, 2021).

The scale of the cultural industry that materialised in the course of the seventeenth century gave rise to a form of power that depended on this distinct form of engineering images – not just sets of them but entire networks of them – that came to form a major aspect of cultural life and daily reality. In this context, prints were not just to be looked at, although this was part of the experience. Rather than constituting mere objects for viewing, they invited forms of dramatic re-enactment. We describe this historical shift, in which new technologies were deployed to make images speak to the public and to one another, thereby technically construing specific forms of individual and collective selves. Images formed an entire infrastructure by means of which people were staging themselves but that also encircled them: a network of images and imaginations that defined their world.

Affectively speaking, the process resulted in a new kind of self, similar to Greenblatt's ground-breaking study on the technical construction of the early modern self: *Renaissance Self-Fashioning* (1980). In scholarly usage, self-fashioning sometimes became a term that indicated the conscious self-presentation of players in a cultural market, as if this self were some sort of *Homo economicus*. Yet Greenblatt's point was that human selves are fundamentally *made* in a complex and dynamic field of practices and discourses (Pieters, 1999; Pieters & Rogiest, 2009). No single subject was, ultimately, in control of or even steering what was happening. This is captured by the term *imagineering* as we used it elsewhere: a verb without a subject. Or, as will become clear in the sections that follow, images could be cut loose from the directive control of political powers through a commercial image market that constantly sought new connections with the institutions of power, aligning itself with regional, national, religious, commercial, republican, royal, private or imperial political programmes and ideologies. Through the print industry, a new visual domain had come to life that manifested itself not only in public space but also in the privacy of homes. Both in the public domain and in the privacy of homes, viewers found themselves taken up in a swirl of images, developing a desire to tap into this experience again and again.

As a present participle that can be turned into a continuous tense, *image engineering* emphasises that it was continuously at work, both externally and internally, in what people saw publicly and what they saw privately, in terms of the machineries that propelled such imaginations and in terms of how people came to behave as a consequence of them. In this context, the making, reproduction and consumption of images were not *about* reality – or not only, in any case. They rather *articulated* the real (Siegert, 2015). The cultural techniques used were aimed at involving onlookers in a more sustained, embodied way, inviting them to enjoy private pleasures or anxieties, which in turn would allow them to be 'taken up' into the reality depicted.

Violence and Its Affordances

The print shown in Figure 9 represents a *Kinder-spel* or children's game. It appears to depict a public, festive manifestation of children playing in the centre of The Hague, the political centre of the Dutch Republic. The print was made

Figure 9 Adriaen van de Venne, *Children's Games*, in Jacob Cats, *Houwelyck*
(Middelburg, Wed. Jan Pietersz. van de Venne, 1625). Rijksmuseum
Amsterdam, RP-P-1937-312.

and published in 1625 and was part of a set of images that were set alongside the
educational poems written by Jacob Cats.

It may seem a coincidence that, among the many games the children are seen
to be engaged in, they are surely also mimicking a military company that
marches across the square to the rhythm of a drum. They do so, moreover,
underneath one kite flying above them and one falling because its string has
been cut. As innocent as the image may appear, the poem underneath the image
sheds a different light. Witness its first stanza:

> Look there upon that paper kite
> That almost touches the heavens on high
> And while the boy pays out the line
> Steadily upward it will climb
> And finally floats up so high,
> that in the end, it's lost from sight.
> But when by accident the string
> On which the kite at first takes wing
> Breaks, oh, that which once stood tall
> Now suddenly has a great fall;
> And there it lies, its vain delight
> Now cruelly mocked with youthful spite,
> What seemed a glorious, wondrous beast
> Leaves dirty paper on the street.

In explaining the image, the text again adds new images. Apparently, the kite string is not only the power that holds the kite up against the wind; it is also the power that ensures that it remains in the air. When the string breaks, the kite floats down and changes from 'wondrous beast' into nothing but 'dirty paper' (Johannes & Leemans, 2020).

Read emblematically, the lines appear to say that he who strives for vanities loses the connection to grounding moral principles and is bound for disaster. The second stanza makes something else explicit, however:

> Like one who, cursed with ambition,
> However high is his position,
> Will always yearn for greater height.
> And never will be satisfied.
> He feeds desires, both foul and fair,
> Until he floats, I know not where;
> But if the vaulting string would break,
> The prop supporting his high state,
> That is the favour of the prince,
> Alas, his head so full of idle wind,
> Once worshipped like a deity
> Will be held up for mockery.

Here, the ambitious, vain man is someone who failed to realise that the prop or pillar of his position does not consist of his own ambition but exists by the grace of the prince. It now becomes telling that the children are playing in The Hague, in the Lange Voorhout, with the house of Johan van Oldenbarnevelt on the left at the back, one of the most important political actors of the young Republic, who had been beheaded just around the corner in 1619, after a show trial set up by stadtholder Maurice of Orange-Nassau. Image and text taken together reflect on the nasty fate of a powerful political actor who had lost the sympathy of the prince. In both the first and the second stanzas, he has turned from being a respected actor into someone who is mocked, from someone who filled the headlines to someone who was trampled on, like filthy paper. Two different domains of the imagination are combined, then: one explicit and upfront, another one implicit; and both connect this print and the text to sets of other images.

The play between the explicit and the implicit will be a recurring theme. For instance, the young Republic was often represented as a tolerant and fragile new state, reluctant to engage in violent action, while at the same time it was a rather aggressive global actor that was quite capable of using violence (see Section 5). One metaphor that aimed to define the young commercial nation was that of the cat: shy and prudent and only violent when attacked by more aggressive animals. The inventor of the metaphor-image, Pieter de la Court, responded to Machiavelli's famous distinction between two modes of exercising power: that of the lion and the fox. In *Interest van Holland: ofte gronden van Holland's Welvaren*, de la Court reconsidered the proverb that a defensive war is one that consumes the one engaging in it. He argued that this proverb was wrong: to him, defensive wars were the only legitimate ones. Yet, with his metaphor of the Dutch Republic as a cat, he again introduced an ambiguous or double set of images that combined the image of a cat shying away with one that would fly at your throat if necessary. So, through the Dutch image market, the young Republic was represented and performed as both a peaceful, joyful entity *and* a violent one.

The market of images helped to glorify Dutch imperial and military power and helped create a sensorial regime in which customers, readers and viewers could attune themselves affectively to a world of violence and enjoyment and be taken up in embodied emotions such as fear, anger, disgust, hate, horror, glory, lust and pride. Focussing on violence, we aim to make clear that this was not just a theme with legal, moral, religious, political or societal implications. Violence offered chances, or it embodied a set of affective affordances. It could be worked smartly by downplaying overly nasty aspects of Dutch violence and suggestively emphasising the violence of others. It offered forms of violence that could be studied in more detail and more depth; to be explored with a wider overview through multiple events; to be combined in a field of associations, with the one shifting into another; to be produced, sold and consumed as a matter of profit and aesthetic experience. The next section will study this dynamic as an instance of desires propelled by distinct economic factors and constituting affective economies.

2 Desire: From Theatrical Accumulation to Deep Spectacle

Desire can be seen as one of the main driving forces behind the affective economy of the commercial Dutch Republic. Entrepreneurs and entertainers increasingly understood the art of triggering desire. Theatres were developing new techniques, raising a new generation of consumers, who, through the consumption of spectacle, came to look for more intense, collective and individualised experiences. Conceptually speaking, desire was elaborately discussed by philosophers such as Spinoza, who in his *Ethics* associated desire primarily with the idea of self-preservation. Desire, for Spinoza, was a specific form of 'appetite'. Whereas appetite defined all bodies as striving bodies, desire was the human awareness of this appetite. The new culture of consumerism tapped into this new self-awareness, as it tried to capture and reshape people's appetites and desires, inviting consumers to understand themselves as desiring individuals.

In this section, we will demonstrate, through the specific case of the Amsterdam Schouwburg, how theatre sought to arouse in the spectator the desire to experience representations as if for real, using violence to create immersive experiences. Throughout the seventeenth century, the theatrical representation of violence became more and more a matter of commercially produced desire. And for this, the theatre – the building itself but also the technologies present in the building – would have to evolve to remain an attractive player in the rapidly growing market of cultural representations.

Theatre As a Cultural Technique

In his preface to *Medea*, the author Jan Vos, the director of the Amsterdam theatre from 1647 to 1667, defended the omnipresence of violence in his tragedies, emphasising at the same time the importance of the credible depiction of violence. In doing so, Vos questioned the Aristotelian poetical paradigm and explicitly presented Seneca as his poetic reference to legitimise his predilection for theatrical horror. The requirement of 'probability' – a central concept of Horace's laws of drama – is historically determined, according to Vos. When he reflects on how Seneca made Medea slaughter her children on stage, Vos contends:

> That Horace could not believe that this imitation could be depicted on stage so vividly as it had happened, is no wonder: of old the Romans [. . .] were used to seeing in their theatres lions, tigers and bears tear apart people, so that the torn intestines, still half alive and dripping with blood, poured out from the murderous wounds on stomach and chest. This made them so cruel at heart, that everything they saw presented otherwise was not believed by them, and therefore hated. So he wrote his laws not for us, but for the Roman playwrights, for I believe that the representation of people being murdered, if shown intensely, can move the feelings of the people by seeing it. (Vos, 1975)

A Roman audience, Vos appears to say, had already seen all forms of horror in the gladiator fights, so the same horror on stage could only be laughable. The Amsterdam audience, on the other hand, is not hampered by this habituation and can therefore be effectively and fully moved by theatrical horror. The depiction of violence in the theatre is thus especially effective in a society where physical violence is regulated by an administrative system of trial and punishment in which new commercial opportunities arise for spectacular representations of violence. Such great commercial successes were achieved by plays with murders, duels or battles. The Spanish theatre in particular suited the taste of the public of the time. Spanish tragedy offered love, honour, revenge, disguises and so on, or more generally 'turmoil' (*woelingen*), the turmoil of the passions but also of the drama itself, with changing identities and plot twists. Yet the theatrical capability to capture the attention of audiences was more than a matter of twists and turns in the plot. It was also a matter of what the theatre was technically capable of.

In 1667, the playwright and theatre director Jan Vos opened the renovated Amsterdam theatre, a *théâtre à l'italienne*. Vos's *Medea* aimed to demonstrate the new possibilities of the theatre, effectively putting his spectacular ambitions into practice. Juxtaposition and accumulation had been the basic dramaturgical principles in the first half of the seventeenth century, when spectacular, violent moments were shown 'horizontally' next to one another, often even within the same period of time. Yet, as the century progressed, the emphasis emphatically shifted to a 'vertical' experience, or an experience in terms of a depth that drew the spectator into the fictional world. With the new theatre it became possible to 'work magic'. The viewing regime within which violence was shown had moved from a horizontal, accumulative theatricality to a more immersive form of spectacle that used depth (Bruyn, 2021).

The first Amsterdam theatre, which had opened in December 1637 with Vondel's *Gijsbrecht van Aemstel*, was rebuilt in the second half of the same century. It opened again in 1665 and offers a well-documented and paradigmatic example of a cultural transformation (Hummelen, 1967; Albach, 1977a, 1977b; Erenstein, 1996; Porteman & Smits-Velt, 2008; Eversmann, 2013). We have five extensively studied images available for the first theatre: a 1658 engraving of the floor plan by Willem van der Laegh; two 1653 engravings by Salomon Savery, showing the view of the stage and the auditorium; a painting by Hans Jurriaensz van Baden, also from 1653, showing the stage from the side of the auditorium during a performance; and, finally, the painting *The Triumph of Folly: Brutus in the Guise of a Fool before King Tarquinius* (1643) by Pieter Jansz Quast (Figure 10).

Quast based his depiction of the scene on P. C. Hooft's description of a series of *tableaux vivants* presented on 5 May 1609 on the occasion of the Twelve-Year Truce, which together tell the story of Brutus's revolt after the rape and suicide of Lucretia (Korsten, 2017: 181). The work demonstrates concisely how

Figure 10 Pieter Quast, *The Triumph of Folly: Brutus in the Guise of a Fool before King Tarquinius* (1643). Mauritshuis, Den Haag.

horizontal theatricality functioned in the early seventeenth century: the *tableau* brings together, at a standstill, various scenes from the course of action and allows the spectator to navigate, as it were, through the story with his gaze. The protagonist in the middle looks at the spectator and thus breaks through the illusion or the fourth wall: he makes the spectator aware of the theatrical construction (Korsten, 2017: 182).

   This first theatre, designed by Jacob van Campen, was, from the perspective of European theatre history, a unique building that brought together different cultural influences and theatrical traditions. Further on in this section we will see how this same infrastructure, however, very quickly reached its own limits. In terms of technical capacity, it responded less and less to the needs of the early modern culture of spectacle. Jan Vos, among others, experienced these limitations at first hand. The rebuilding and furnishing of the theatre by Philip Vingboons in 1665 was a response to a cultural and economic development that had already been going on for some time. From that moment on, Amsterdam had a fully fledged spectacle machine at its disposal. This machine offered new possibilities for responding more efficiently to the spectators' desires or, more so, for producing these desires and then exploiting them commercially. The omnipresence of violent representations in the theatre of that period (though violence is not the only spectacular effect exploited) and the horror they initiated are an integral part of this growing affective economy, with the desire for spectacle as one of the driving forces.

Accumulation and Juxtaposition

In 1648, the year of the Peace of Münster, the Spanish tragi-comedy *De beklaagelycke dwang* (*The Pitiful Coercion*) had its premiere, a translation and adaptation of *La fuerza lastimosa* by the Spanish author Félix Lope de Vega (Vega, 1648). The actor and playwright Isaac Vos was responsible for the adaptation, which was based on an intermediate prose translation by Jacob Barocas. *De beklaagelycke dwang* was to become one of the big successes of the Amsterdam theatre. It was a typical Spanish baroque play: complicated love intrigues, betrayals and misunderstandings, cross-dressing, changes of location, jumps in time, ruses and violence continually postponed, including executions only just averted and a duel as the dramatic climax of a complicated story built on false accusations and a multitude of actions and passions. The many plot twists that succeeded each other in a play such as *De beklaagelycke dwang* connected seamlessly with the 'changes of state' (*staatveranderingen*) of the characters: they were hurled from one frame of mind to another, from one emotion to another, from one social status to another 'like a rudderless ship at sea' (Blom & Marion, 2021: 29). In short, this is a play full of 'turmoil' (*woelingen*). With the constant changes in time and space, the authors not only capitalised on the public's desire to be constantly surprised; the narrative instability inherent in these plays perfectly symbolises the instability of the baroque world view.

In his preface, Isaac Vos emphasises that the play is in keeping with the spirit of the age: 'it seems to me [...] incongruous, in the rhyming of plays for the present time, to pay attention to the past; now that the eye, as well as the ears, wants to have a share in what is shown to it' (Blom & Marion, 2021: 29). The adaptation by Vos is a telling example of the 'hispanisation' of the Dutch stage from the 1640s onwards. Indeed, recent research describes how important authors such as Lope de Vega and Pedro Calderon de la Barca were for the Amsterdam theatre (Blom & Marion, 2021: 67). For the first period of the theatre, between 1638 and 1672, Blom and van Marion count 43 Spanish plays in the repertoire, often quite spectacular and violent plays, with *Sigismundus, Prinçe van Poolen* (after Calderon's *Het leven een droom*) as the big success, with 133 performances.

The complicated narrative structure of *The Pitiful Coercion* runs as follows. The love of the couple Dionysia, daughter of the English king, and Henryck, a count, is thwarted by the courtier Octavio. The latter disguises himself as

Henryck and spends a sweet night with the crown princess. Henryck, for his part, waits for his beloved in vain and leaves desperate. Octavio's deception leads Henryck to think that Dionysia has betrayed him (the court is full of rumours about the princess's night of love), and she in turn thinks that her lover has left her because he has fled to his original wife Rosaura. The audience watches everything happen, knows the true facts (having witnessed Octavio's ruse) and sees how a spiral of shame, false accusations and revenge unfolds. When the king (for the audience obviously hinting at his own daughter) asks Henryck what he would do with a man of lower rank who leaves a crown princess for his wife after a night of love, the latter condemns himself to death with his answer: 'by the murder of his wife; in punishment of his evil and wicked deed' (Vega, 1671: 42, quoted in Blom, 2021: 238). The audience then knows how things stand. Henryck's wife, Rosaura, however, will come to her husband's rescue: she will sacrifice herself. Henryck, however, cannot cope with that and sends her out to sea.

The scene between the third and fourth acts shows Rosaura floating at sea in a small boat. Rosaura then disguises herself as a servant – before 1655, when the first female actresses enter the stage, the audience thus sees a man playing a woman disguised as a man. In the final scene, the moment of the execution of (a blindfolded) Henryck has arrived. When the sword is about to strike, Rosaura steps forward, disguised as a guard, to reveal the true cause of all the misunderstandings and expose Octavio as the guilty party. A duel ensues between Rosaura (still in disguise) and Octavio, who does not want to be insulted by a servant. Octavio wounds his opponent, who is brought down but still breathing, whereupon Vos inserts the following dialogue between the bystanders on stage:

> Alt(enio): Oh, no, there is still life there.
>
> Fab(io): Depart, my lord, depart, and please give him breathing space /
> Untie his bosom. So, alright now, I trust / it will get better.
>
> Klen(ardo): Oh wonder! It's a woman.
>
> Cel(inde): In fact, it's Rozaura, my hope is deceived.
>
> (Vega, 1671: 77)

Clearly, with such a wide range of characters, disguises and twelve musketeers, the play 'switches' constantly by fluctuations and turns that together represent the 'turmoil' or capriciousness of baroque existence.

Whereas in de Vega's version a number of things are revealed only through the characters' discourse, Vos adds three performances accompanied by music (Blom, 2021: 234–47), a series of visual effects, including a *tableau* (non-existent in the Spanish tradition) and a duel. The audience's attention must be fed with ever-new twists. This accumulative dramaturgy fitted in perfectly with the possibilities but also the limitations that the Amsterdamse Schouwburg had to offer at that time (Bruyn, 2021).

The Amsterdam theatre of 1637, where *De beklaagelycke dwang* had its premiere, was 'a curious mixture of old-fashioned and modern' (Hummelen, 1996: 202). Its circular form was reminiscent of the Elizabethan theatre. Just as in the French *jeu-de-paume* theatre, there was no strict separation between the stage and the audience. At the same time, the floor plan suggests the Italian influence of Palladio's Teatro Olympico in the northern Italian town of Vincenza. The influence of the rhetorician theatre, with the system of the 'open camer', is also unmistakable. The architect van Campen explicitly fell back on Roman models for his design, which allowed him to draw a parallel between Amsterdam and Rome. This parallel was also picked up by Vondel in his foreword to the play *Gysbreght*:

> We imitate the great Rome in miniature,
> Now that Kampen is building,
> And reaches for heaven with wood and stone.
>
> (Vondel, 1929: 526)

The classical arrangement of the theatre suggested a certain degree of equality between the citizens, fitting in nicely with the self-image of Amsterdam as the epicentre of a self-confident bourgeoisie. Significantly, though, van Campen would add two rows of boxes to his Roman inspiration, providing a space for the burgeoning commercial elite to distinguish itself socially and spatially from the rest of the public.

Van Campen provided a semi-circular auditorium with a 16-metre-wide stage (Figure 11). The auditorium was surrounded by galleries that faced the parterre rather than the stage (Figure 12). The stage is organised horizontally – that is, in breadth rather than in depth (Figure 13). At the back of the stage there was a removable rear wall with a system of screens, turning the stage into a flexible instrument, which allowed the theatrical space to be adapted to various types of play (Kuyper, 1970; Hummelen, 1996; Erenstein, 1996). The polytopic model made it possible to present action in different places on the same stage at the same time. That same stage could also be transformed into a monotopic space via the screens. The wide, horizontal stage opening fitted in perfectly with the accumulative structure of the play: the spectators could let their gaze navigate over a synthetic representation of the action. A play such as *De beklaagelycke dwang* fits in perfectly with this theatrical space: van Campen's model made it possible to bring

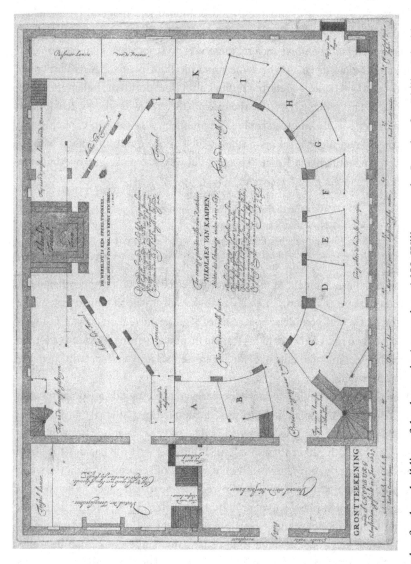

Figure 11 Floor plan for the rebuilding of the theatre in Amsterdam, 1658. Willem van der Laegh, after Philips Vinckboons (II), after Jacob van Campen, 1658 engraving. Rijksmuseum Amsterdam, RP-P-OB-46.816.

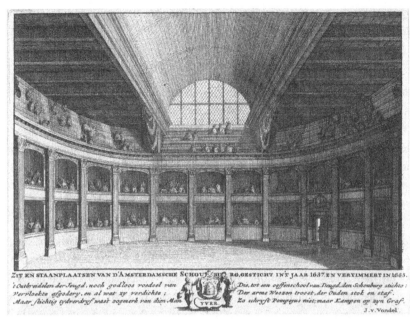

Figure 12 Auditorium of the 1637 Amsterdam theatre on the Keizersgracht. Rijksmuseum Amsterdam, RP-P-OB-81.423.

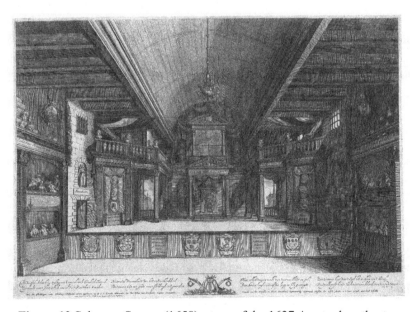

Figure 13 Salomon Savery (1658), stage of the 1637 Amsterdam theatre. Rijksmuseum Amsterdam, RP-P-OB-70.100.

together a wide range of characters on stage and to navigate smoothly from one intrigue to another.

Immersion and Depth

The new theatre opened in 1667 with the appearance of the sorceress Medea on its stage. The choice of this play was no coincidence: the abundance of violent scenes required new techniques which would have been impossible to show in the old theatre. The new theatre and its spectacular machinery enabled sorcery through the creation of immense, credible experiences and the use of a perspective of depth. In this context, the character of Medea may be perceived as the symbolic start of a new theatrical regime.

Jan Vos published his version of *Medea* with the telling subtitle *Treurspel met Konst- en Vliegh-werken* (*Tragedy with Artifice and Airborne Techniques*; 1667). That same year, the sorceress Medea appeared for the second time, in Lodewijk Meijer's *Gulden Vlies* (*Golden Fleece*), which added a good deal of spectacular effects. The play by Jan Vos reads like a programme statement. Not only did he put his personal poetics into practice; he also showed what the theatre could achieve as a new dream machine. Vos presented Medea as a force of nature, from a foreign country, defying all laws. Just as Medea is not constrained by the limitations of reality, Jan Vos sets aside the limitations of the outdated theatrical regime. He performed magic not only with the character of Medea but with reality itself. Explicit theatricality thus made way for magical immersion.

In his *Medea*, Vos opts for fierce violence, with the fourth act its undoubted climax. Medea, 'on a chariot pulled through the air by two fire-breathing dragons' (Vos, 1667: 55), throws her children from the chariot, smashing them on the stage:

> Iaz.: O give me my children, hear how thy Jazon flatters.
> Med.: There are thy children: is Jazon now flattered?
>   (She flies with the chariot into the air, and throws the children on
>   the ground; the ghosts sink.)
> Iaz.: I hear, O gods, I hear their skulls cracking.

> (Vos, 1667: 58)

Vos makes eager use of the possibilities of the depth of the new stage and the machinery offered by the new theatre. He has Medea change the pleasure garden of the first act into a wild mountain landscape, 'Here the pleasure garden, at the stamping of her foot, must turn into mountains' (Vos, 1667: 28), and then back again: 'Here the mountains turn into a pleasure garden again' (Vos, 1667: 28). In this way, Vos introduced the audience to the coulisse theatre, which made it possible to replace one scene with another, as if the theatre were a slide projector – in contrast to the spatial and dramaturgical stacking of the old theatre. In the same act, Medea turns the two guards into a tree and a pillar:

> O gods! What's happening? I do not know how to react:
> My limbs stiffen. I will take reve . . . .
> *He turns into a pillar.* (Vos 1667: 5)

And still, it is not enough. Because the guards keep talking, to Medea's great irritation, she changes them into a bear and a tiger. And so, Medea becomes the mirror image of Vos's poetics: unbridled, untameable, a force of magic and artifice.

The need for a new theatre in Amsterdam, less than four decades after the first one opened, seems to have been informed by the growing interest in immersive theatrical experiences. According to one of the theatre directors, the old theatre was 'much too wide and short', and 'because of its heaviness and solidity, it cannot be quickly and easily changed time and again, easily, according to the demands of the play' (Domselaer, 1665: 207, quoted in Blom, 2021: 354). The new theatre should be able to 'work magic' by expanding its technical capacity through the architecture of the building and the integration of new theatrical techniques. The design by Philip Vingboons followed the latest trends in European, specifically Italian, theatre architecture. It was informed by Nicola Sabbatini's famous *Pratica di fabricar scene e machine ne' teatri* (1638), which circulated widely in Europe and provided many designers with the blueprint for their new theatres. The Roman-inspired semi-circular auditorium, with its wide, short stage, was replaced by a horseshoe-shaped hall with a deep-winged stage. The auditorium and stage were separated by a stage arch, with a spacious orchestra pit. The proscenium could be closed off with a curtain. In contrast to the old theatre, the new model was aimed at an individual viewing experience. The spectators were invited to immerse themselves in the peepshow reality that unfolded on stage. The new design thus can be seen as an attempt to transform the stage into an autonomous reality through monotopic spatiality.

Spectators no longer entered from the side but from the back. The parterre (*bak*) held ten rows of benches. At the back there were a limited number of standing places. The cheap seats were located at the top. The regents' loge, accessible from the regents' room, was close to the stage and offered an ideal view of the scene. Vingboons's design thus brought the Republic in line with other European, monarchical regimes, whereby the theatrical reality was adapted to the perspective of a sovereign (*l'oeil du prince*) and the spectator space was hierarchically arranged according to the distance from that ideal perspective (Surgers, 2009; Hewitt, 1958).

At the opening of the new theatre on 26 May 1665, Jan Vos had an allegorical poem performed in dialogue form, entitled 'Inauguration of the Theatre of Amsterdam'. In that poem he not only highlighted the social, educational and charitable function of the theatre but especially praised the new technical possibilities, presenting them to the reader to arouse the spectator's desire to see the same techniques used more extensively in other plays: 'Here one sees the sea and the beach, surrounded by steep mountains. [. . .] Now you see tents, which surround a large city [. . .] Here art shows a forest in which the light never shines. [. . .] Here a building, full of glory, is shown to you' (Amir, 1996: 258). The new theatre offered a whole range of new techniques, some of which were depicted in van Frankendaal's print (Figure 14): seven trapdoors for appearances and disappearances, a machine for a raging sea, the possibility of working with fire and smoke, and especially a series of 'flying works'. In *Medea*, Jan Vos used a 'heavenly globe', a flying cloud in which actors could travel:

> Here a celestial globe, decorated with stars, descends from the heavenly vault, and opens in eight pieces, out of which the seven planets, each shown according to its own characteristics, appear, which, after dancing, go back into the globe, which closes up and disappears upwards. (Vos, 1667: 51–2)

The perspective sets replaced the horizontal stage design of the old theatre. The linen backdrops were painted by famous artists such as Gerard de Lairesse and could be quickly moved on and off the stage via grooves in the stage floor. They made it possible to change the scene from one reality to another at lightning speed. The seven trapdoors facilitated rapid transformations: magic thus became possible. The new theatre offered the possibility to overwhelm the spectator with a continuous change (instead of a juxtaposition) of theatrical spaces. In other words, the audience was immersed in a new fiction with every change of setting. While the old theatre used mimetic codes that together formed an implicit agreement between the artist and the spectator, in the new theatre one could be taken up into another world. The new theatre provided the instruments for a search that had already begun decades before: away from theatrical convention, towards more illusion, from theatrical 'showing' towards spectacular 'overwhelming'.

A World in Permanent Motion

The renovation of the Amsterdam theatre and the way in which, among other things, violence was depicted reflect a more profound mutation of techniques of visualisation over the course of the seventeenth century: from breadth to depth, from frontal to perspectival, from polytopic to monotopic, from demonstration to immersion, from juxtaposition to change. The theatrical regime in van Campen's

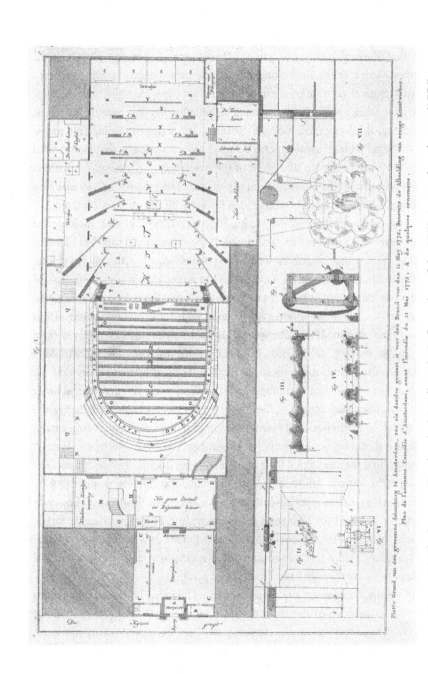

Figure 14 Nicolaas van Frankendaal (attributed to), floor plan of the 1772 Amsterdam theatre (1774). Rijksmuseum Amsterdam, RP-P-OB-84.752.

theatre can be labelled exhibitionist, as it explicitly emphasises the theatrical and, hence, constructed nature of the events on display. The new theatre approached the spectator as a voyeur, enchanted by a dream world. The spectator was presented with the illusion of being alone. From this solitude, a privileged view of another, illusory, reality was gained. This is perhaps why Jan Vos chose the sorceress Medea as the first protagonist in the new theatre. In van Campen's theatre, theatrical convention defines the contract between stage and spectator through the latter's willing suspension of disbelief; in the new theatre, the magic of theatrical illusion would trick the spectator into a dream world. This magic tried to trigger an individual experience, even though we know that the material reality itself of the theatre (the noise of the machinery, for example) remained a major obstacle to this individualised experience. The gradual individualisation of the spectator experience is taken a step further with the *rarekiek* (Section 3).

Behind the renovation of the theatre, deeper ideological and sociological shifts were hidden. In the old theatre, the spectators together formed a community, whose members were more or less equal. After all, everyone had an equally good or equally bad view of the stage. The arrangement was not based on an ideal perspective. This does not imply that the old theatre lacked the means for sociological stratification. Those with more money could afford a place in the surrounding gallery and thus could distinguish themselves from the plebs in the 'pit'. In the new, perspectivist theatre, only the regents' loge offered an ideal view of the theatrical reality. This infrastructure divided the audience into socio-economic subgroups according to a strict hierarchical order which was translated spatially: the higher up the social ladder, the better the view of the theatrical fiction. This mutation might illustrate the changing way in which the Republic, and especially Amsterdam's rulers, saw themselves. It illustrated how they imagined their political power: from *assemblée* (in accordance with the antique references in the old theatre accurately mapped out by Eversmann) to sociological hierarchisation. The new theatre building was a perfect instrument for bourgeois governmentality. The infrastructure forced its users to internalise the social stratification. This new technology created a new kind of self – that of the individual spectator – and also invited that spectator to internalise his or her own social position.

And yet the above assumption deserves some nuance, if one takes the reality of the social practice of theatre – that is, how it actually worked (or did not work) in the auditorium – as the starting point for the material reality of theatre history. In reality, different regimes coexisted within one and the same cultural practice, both in the old theatre and in the new: public theatricality on the one hand and spectacular immersion on the other. The transition to a new theatrical regime should not be seen as a radical break or the beginning of a new paradigm

(Elenbaas, 2004). The monotopic scenography was already being experimented with in the old theatre (Kuyper, 1970: 100). Conversely, the popularity of *tableaux* deep into the eighteenth century forces us to nuance the hypothesis of evolution from a horizontal to a perspectival theatricality. The seventeenth-century theatre space is thus a hybrid space in which different regimes coexist. The new theatre does not really mark a radical break but should be regarded as the result of a gradual transition from a polytopic, horizontal theatricality to a monotopic, 'deep' spectacularity.

Still, throughout the seventeenth century, a number of new techniques were developed in the theatre which enabled the new professionals of the spectacle industry to arouse desires in the spectators more efficiently and to subsequently make these desires 'imaginable'. In the early modern theatre culture of the Dutch Republic, different desires converged, with violence as a flywheel. The theatre catered to the desire for spectacle, for magic, for intense experiences and for the confrontation with unknown realities. As a cultural technique, the Amsterdam theatre was quite successful in arousing this desire, precisely by implicating the spectators more and more in the performance. The spectator no longer primarily contemplated, together with the other spectators. In the violent effects that accumulated in the new theatre, in a play such as *Medea*, the spectator literally saw the theatrical reality change before his or her eyes.

The promise of a constantly transforming theatrical reality made it possible to produce ever-new desires. This instability is crucial in economic terms: the theatre presented performances that could constantly change and therefore always arouse new curiosity. The new theatre was urged to constantly create these new desires to remain economically profitable. The essence of early modern theatre as a cultural technique was therefore not so much the illusion of what was being shown but the suggestion of a world in permanent motion, a continuous process of appearance and disappearance, and this via a script imposed on spectators who followed a plot while having the feeling of exploring, travelling and immersing themselves in other worlds.

Moreover, the spectacle machine exploited a social desire – namely, the desire to have been there, to be amazed, shocked or moved by the imagined fiction, and at the same time to share the same social time-space with other spectators. It is this dual effect that the engineering of imageries aimed to achieve: to include the spectator in a visually connected whole, to make spectators dream about a reality that they cannot (yet) see that lies hidden somewhere in the depths of the theatrical illusion. Throughout the seventeenth century, the theatre thus contributed to the growth of a market for violent imagination, in which, just like the printing industry, it always emphatically pursued a privatisation and massification of the experience and exploited it commercially. The Amsterdam case provided a telling illustration of how, in the course of the seventeenth century, the theatre was reinvented as a marketplace where the collective desire for individual, personalised experiences was both produced and satisfied. Spectators were trained to want to experience intense horror. The theatre, as a cultural technique, stimulated that desire.

3 Interest: Collective Self-Interest Construed and Contested

What is the role of *interest* in the affective economy of violence in the early modern Dutch Republic? Different equivalents in seventeenth-century Dutch for 'interest' had strong negative connotations associated with the concept of egoism, as in the case of *eigenbaat*: the interest of the self. In the second half of the seventeenth century, however, more positive connotations were added to the notion of self-interest (Hirschman, 1977), especially due to Spinozism with its emphasis on *conatus*, the drive towards self-preservation (Gatens & Lloyd, 1999: 27). In both cases, interest was considered an *affect*. This affective approach also characterised political and economic interpretations of the word, as in the influential publication *Interest of Holland* (1662) by the de la Court brothers. Here 'interest' refers to the collective Dutch striving for wealth and prosperity based on what these authors saw as the nation's longing for economic and political freedom. As has been shown elsewhere by Leemans (2021b), interest as a moral and political term in the Dutch Republic balanced common interest and the passions of self-love, coming together in the Dutch word *belang*. In allegorical representation, for instance, *belang* is often depicted as a personification of the common good (*gemenebest*), which means that the collective longing for wealth cannot do without an individual figure that embodies this very concept.

The relationship and possible tensions between self-interest and collective interests will be further explored in this section by focussing on conflicts of interest and the violence resulting from them or the other way round: violence *as* a collective interest. This will be done through the lens of embodiment, reflecting on how the representation of violence could construe collective bodies of interest, how it could stage conflicts between bodies of interest and how the applied visualising techniques could evoke interest and curiosity, both individually and collectively, regarding the topic of violence (Figure 15).

Invested Interests, Splendid Confusion: Fireworks As Constructions of Unity

Local and regional authorities in the Dutch Republic had a great interest in organising public celebrations after the signing of a peace treaty. They often used these celebrations to position themselves as peacemakers with sufficient

Figure 15 Laurens Scherm (around 1702, or 1725–33), *Riot on the Dam Square and Looting Mob in 1696*. Rijksmuseum Amsterdam, RP-P-OB-82.871.

power (in Dutch: *geweld*, a term also used for force or violence) to enforce a peace. These political interests were closely intertwined with a religious discourse on peace and unity. The political and religious celebrations took place during 'days of thanksgiving and prayer' (*dank- en bededagen*), after the proclamation of a new peace. The religious part was central to these celebrations, with sermons about the peace and giving thanks to God through prayers. The secular government supplemented these religious festivities with public manifestations of gratitude and joy, the fixed element being the lighting of bonfires on the towers and in the streets and the firing of salutes. Fireworks also became a regular part of these peace celebrations from the seventeenth century onwards.

The celebration of a peace treaty by means of fireworks connected that same peace with military violence through the medium itself. The pyrotechnologies with which fireworks were made were military in origin. Recreational fireworks were developed at courts in the sixteenth century and became a more wide-spread, professionalised phenomenon in the seventeenth century. Early hand-books on fireworks frequently refer to this military origin, as in *La pyrotechnie* (1630) by Hanzelet Lorrain, which has the motto 'Marte et Arte' on its title page. The book describes various machines and 'artifices de feux' that can be used 'pour la Guerre & Recreation'. The basic syntax of these early recreational fireworks was, according to Kevin Salatino (1997: 40), strongly linked to the 'language of war'. This language of war consisted of all kinds of military elements in festive fireworks, from warships to complete re-enactments of city sieges as part of the firework display.

The connection with the military is also evident from the interests that were involved in the context of the Dutch war policy of the time. The celebration of peace through fireworks had to show the Dutch population that the military power of the Dutch state displayed during the now ended war had to serve the prosperity of the Republic and its inhabitants. The ultimate goal of the peace celebrations was to strengthen a sense of unity and community. For these reasons, the date of a day of thanksgiving and prayer was fixed for the whole nation, so that it would be celebrated everywhere at the same time (Rooden, 1992: 704–5; Frijhoff, 1996: 18–24). The simultaneity of the celebrations expressed a sense of unity, a feeling that had to be spread to all layers of society through attractive public events. Such a sense of unity was all the more import-ant for a state that at the end of the seventeenth century was strongly divided culturally, politically and religiously, with constant tensions between, for example, radical republicans and the Organists (who were in support of the stadtholderate) but also between the different faiths in the Republic and frictions within the Dutch Reformed Church itself (see Frijhoff & Spies, 2004: chaps. 2 & 6; Israel, 1998: chap. 27).

At the end of the Nine Years' War (1688–97), the political discord in the Dutch Republic reached a new peak due to a conflict of interests that occurred both in the political arena and on the streets, especially in Amsterdam. The high costs of the war against France weighed on the city's treasury and trade, which also had an effect on the city's population, especially the lower classes. As the largest city of the Dutch Republic's wealthiest province of Holland, Amsterdam had to contribute significantly to the costs of the war (Haven, 2004: 315). High taxes ensued, and a new tax on marriage and burials threw the fat on the fire:

a major riot broke out in the city in January 1696. It was the well-known 'Aansprekersoproer' (Undertakers' Riot), to which we will return in the section 'Conflicting Interests, Solidarity and Division: Rioting Bodies on the Street'. Historians assume that this riot was also related to war fatigue on the part of the population of Amsterdam (cf. Porta, 1975: 12; Kurtz, 1928: 210). One of the riot's main targets was (the house of) Burgomaster Boreel, who was not only the initiator of the new taxes but also Amsterdam's negotiator in the long diplomatic run-up to the Peace of Ryswick (1697).

This Peace of Ryswick came as a great gift to Amsterdam's political elite. The burgomasters could use the peace to treat the population to a public celebration on 6 November 1697 after the difficult years that lay behind. The peace policy, as it had been practised in the years preceding the treaty, had taken place behind the screens. Now that the treaty was signed, the news should be made public, with the people of Amsterdam playing the desired role of the grateful recipient of the peace. The celebration of peace became part of an urban and politicised 'gift economy' at a macro level: the city council granted the population 'peace' with entertaining fireworks; the population gave gratitude, unity and loyalty in return. The 'gift economy' thus realised aimed to transform the previously divided population of Amsterdam into an undivided 'body of interest' that gratefully received the peace granted, instead of questioning the politics of the city council.

The idea of giving and receiving recurs at various moments in early modern peace celebrations. Most clearly and explicitly, this was done through a practice that came from the world of the court and diplomacy, such as when the people were treated to free wine. For example, during the celebration of the Peace of Breda (1667) in The Hague, various wine foun-tains were set up in the streets that attracted a lot of people trying to fill their glasses with wine. In one of the depictions (Figure 16), the wine pours forth from the arrows of the Dutch lion (see Section 2 about that imagery), which are transformed into small wine fountains. Instead of symbolising the mili-tary strength of the seven states, the lion's arrows now express the material abundance that peace will bring the population. The arrows also, of course, express direction and strength – a purpose previously referring to violence in times of war and now referring to how 'peace and prosperity' are poured over the population.

For the festivities on 6 November 1697, there is no mention of wine fountains in the reports, but there were some pyrotechnic spectacles to enjoy in several cities. According to a report in the *Amsterdamse Courant* (7 November 1697), the pedestal depicted the battle between Bellona, Mars and the peace. One side of the pedestal was devoted to the benefits of the peace; the other side to the gods

1.*Huysen vande Ambassadeurs der Hoogm.H.ᵗᵉ Staten.* 2.*Staken met Picktonnen.*
3.*Den Leeuw met seven Pylen, alwaer de wyn overvloedigh uyt vloeyde.*

Figure 16 Romeyn de Hooghe (1667), detail from *Vreede-handelingh tot Breda*. Rijksmuseum Amsterdam, RP-P-1885-A-9009.

of war, depicting the horrors of war. Next to the throne of Mars, the spectator could see burning houses, while civilians gathered in front of his throne, being forced to pay for the war: 'pouring out their bags full of gold and silver before the throne' (*Amsterdamse Courant*, 7 November 1697). These fiery representations highlight the financial pains suffered by citizens in the business of war, as taxpayers, although they also represent the military horrors of war quite explicitly. In this way, the financial suffering that the war had caused to the civic body of Amsterdam becomes one of its horrors, which should strengthen positive feelings among Amsterdam's population towards those who brought peace and unity to the country.

It is hard to believe that the political message these fireworks had to transmit was their most entertaining aspect. It was the pyrotechnic spectacle that fascinated early modern onlookers. Fireworks were an intrinsically baroque genre, and their overwhelming effect had to ensure that the 'eye got lost in it', according to the *Description of the Beautiful Fireworks* (*Beschryving van het Prachtig Vuurwerk*),[1] which reported on the fireworks that were organised by the Amsterdam magistrate for Russian delegates on 29 August 1697. The effect

---

[1] *Beschryving van het Prachtig Vuurwerk, 't geen door ordre der Ed. Magistraat van de Stad Amsterdam op den 29sten Augustus 1697 ter eere van het GROOT MUSKOVISCH GESANTSCHAP, aangesteeken is.* Amsterdam: Allard, 1697.

Figure 17 Romeyn de Hooghe, fireworks organised in Antwerp to celebrate the Peace of Ryswick. *Olyven-krans*, Antwerpen 1697. Rijksmuseum Amsterdam, RP-P-OB-76.321.

of disorder and confusion that fireworks had to create was part of their 'grandeur'. A firework is 'truly grand', that is, precisely because of its 'splendid confusion' – as Edmund Burke would put it sixty years later in his famous treatise on the sublime (Salatino, 1997: 3, 48).

An emotion that belongs to the sublime, and certainly also to fireworks, is the short moment of fear and fright caused by such a dangerous spectacle. In prints, such as the one in Figure 17, we regularly see a frightened audience recoiling from the dangerous scene, which is not an unreasonable response given that early modern fireworks regularly caused deaths. The moment of fear, 'disorder' and 'splendid confusion' shown in Figure 17 would have its 'orderly release' in what came after the fireworks: the retrospective description of the events in the newspapers that often tried to reconstruct the right order of the fireworks that was imperceptible during the performance itself.

The poems that accompanied the fireworks and festivities regularly refer to the sense of unity and togetherness that needed to be experienced by the celebrating population during the peace celebrations, as well as, of course, the gratitude towards the government and to God that was central to the message of these thanksgiving days. The pamphlet *Zee en Land-triomf over de Vreede* (*Sea and*

Land Triumph about the Peace), for example, depicts the collective joy about the peace that prevails among the population, referring to the element of 'fire' as a sign of that joy. It is obvious that 'fire' refers to the use of pyrotechnics, but it also refers to the emotions experienced by the viewer who is 'inwardly burning / of divine fire' that was kindled by peace.[2] The satisfaction of the population is clearly charged with emotions here. Peace is given by God and sets hearts on fire; it fills the population with strong emotions of happiness and contentment. The fire of war (pyrotechnics) that is used to organise a fire of peace (the festive fireworks) now becomes an inner fire that fills the citizens with contentment and gratitude.

Although the martial peace fireworks might seem to be a 'voluntary gift' from the authorities, then, without too many obligations on the part of the recipient, there was a clear 'obligation to receive' and to repay the received gift (Mauss, 1970: 10–11; Graeber, 2001: 225). This supposed repayment concerns the internal social peace that the city council hoped to receive after the turbulent years leading up to the peace. Theatrical entertainment was the reward here for the burden of the war. Something similar held for the regular theatre. The theatre was closed during wartime, as well as in times of riot and social unrest, and was reopened afterwards, as we will see in the case of the 'Aansprekersoproer'. So, the 'pleasant pastime' of theatre and fireworks, instituted by the city, was certainly not 'without obligation' on the part of the population. The celebrations had to safeguard the existing social and political order. The fireworks were supposed to be a reward for the efforts of the citizens to remain silent in times of war and social unrest, giving in return their tacit assent to the power and wealth accumulated by the urban elite that governed the city.

Absorption and Involvement: War As a Peepshow

Prints of fireworks mostly appeared in magazines, such as the quarterly *Europische Mercurius* that reported on international diplomacy and politics. In one of the issues of 1697, a print by Laurens Scherm depicted one of the three big firework displays organised in The Hague on the occasion of the Peace of Ryswick on 6 November 1697 (Figure 18). The print was accompanied by a fairly extensive explanation of the firework display and its visual programme.

Rather than fulfilling a need for political interpretation (in terms of what it was all about), the print, first and foremost, offers visual entertainment. These aims seem to be contradictory. The print emphasises the pyrotechnic spectacle that obscures the iconographic details of the scaffolding and pedestals that are central to the accompanying description. Yet, in combination with the detailed

---

[2] *Zee en Land-triomf over de Vreede, gesloten tot Ryswyk op den 20 en 21 Sept.* Amsterdam: Jacobus Robyn, 1697.

Figure 18 Laurens Scherm, fireworks organised in The Hague
(6 November 1697) by the States General and the States of Holland and West-
Friesland to celebrate the Peace of Ryswick in honour of the stadtholder-king
William III (*Europische Mercurius* 1697, pp. 362–3). Rijksmuseum
Amsterdam, RP-P-OB-76.320.

description, it highlights the already mentioned tension between spectacular
representation in which 'the eye gets lost' and the desire to focus on each single
detail of the fireworks' imagery.

The prints and descriptions in pamphlets and newspapers reproduced the
visual spectacle (Frijhoff, 2015), but they also enabled the audience to read the
political message of the fireworks more carefully. That is, the depiction of
the fireworks managed to combine the sublime experience with their political
message. In the image in Figure 18, for instance, despite the apparently chaotic
representation of a criss-cross of lines that represent arrows and explosions, we
still discern a kind of symmetry in the depiction. This symmetry also character-
ises the structure of the original fireworks and supports a hierarchy of meanings.
The flashes of the rockets recede in the centre of the etching to reveal the central
allegorical figures and initials. The first are Vesta and Neptune, referring to land
and sea trade. They sit on the pedestal in the middle. This also shows the initials
of the king-stadtholder: 'WR' – that is, William Rex. The same applies to the
central parts of the two temples on either side of the pedestal, which are
illuminated by explosions behind each of its allegorical figures that represent
abstract concepts such as freedom, peace and prosperity.

Firework prints were the ideal objects to be shown in illuminated viewing
boxes of the seventeenth and eighteenth centuries. An example of this is a print

of a firework display on the occasion of the Treaty of Utrecht in 1713 (Figure 19). By lighting up specific parts of the print with coloured transparent paper strips, the spectacle of the fireworks as well as the allegorical scenes on the pedestal are highlighted. These highlighted parts invite the audience to have a closer look at the allegorical details of the depiction, enjoy the details and understand their political meaning.

Viewing boxes were a popular medium from the late seventeenth century onwards to show these kinds of spectacular engravings to a broader audience, which could thus obtain a glimpse 'inside the box'. The name of these boxes emphasises the element of interest and curiosity of the viewing public. They were called 'moy fraay curieux', which means something like 'a fine wonderful curiosity' through which spectators could obtain a glance of unknown worlds 'beyond one's self' (Balzer, 1998: 12). Some of these boxes were used for travelling peepshows. Through a refined system of mirrors and lenses, showmen of the early peepshows could rapidly change between scenes by pulling a string with tape connected to the top of the print to manipulate the views. Apart from changing scenes, the showmen also had the opportunity to draw the viewer's attention to details of the scene by elaborating on them when commenting on the scenes for the audience. The experience of the peepshow thus comes close to the twofold

Figure 19 Daniel Stoopendaal, illumination print of the fireworks organised in The Hague to celebrate the Peace of Utrecht in 1713 (*Afbeeldingh van het Theater met syn ornamenten en Constigh Vuurwerck*). Private collection.

experience described for fireworks: the spectacle in which the eye 'gets lost' comes to be combined with the detailed description through an accompanying text that explains the spectacle to the viewer in all its details. The two together work to gain the audience's interest. Thus, the peep into the box confronts the viewer with a whirling show of different scenes, a swirl that is fascinating by itself, because the viewer does not know where to look in the first instance but, on the other hand, is also forced to take a closer look at details that demand attention based on the comments of the showman.

One of the earliest Dutch accounts of a travelling peepshow is at an Amsterdam fair that presented a cumulative spectacle of images about war, slaughter and rape (*De Tweede Amsterdamse Posttyding*)[3] (cf. Nieuwenhuis, 2016). If we can believe the fictional account from around 1688, the showman 'Jean' explains the scenes with an explicit reference to the atrocities in the 'Disaster Year' 1672:

> Here you see the fire and devastation of Swammerdam and Bodegraven,
> Here the Frenchman is plundering, here they throw children on the fire,
> Here they violate the women, here a man is killed.
> Alarm, alarm, here is horror and fright.[4]

The repetition of 'here' refers both to the swift change of scenes and to certain elements of the scene to which the viewer should pay special attention (names of places, the victims, the way of killing), eliciting an interest in these scenes. Such selected horror scenes might well have been taken from the de Hooghe prints of the French atrocities mentioned in Section 2.

In this case, the viewer 'Jeannetje' responds in a resigned way. Not enjoying seeing the different pictures of 'murder and fire', she asks for an end to all these horrors.[5] Trying to escape the horrific peepshow, she indirectly admits that the successive performance of all these shocking images in the 'intimate' small wooden box has an overwhelming effect on the onlooker, who vacillates between wanting to see more and looking away.

The commercial peepshows were not immediately spectacular themselves. They catered to the curious eye of both collectives and the individual, a combination captured by the fact that the act of looking in the box was a public act. The viewer, however, was also invited to interact by engaging with the dramatist, or the 'showman' (Balzer, 1998: 26–8). In many cases the peepshow showed scenes of mass violence, as in battlefield scenes. The viewer would be part of a group of people, the group that visited, for instance, the fair

---

[3] *De tweede Amsterdamse posttyding moy fraay curieux van de keuninke van Vrankryke, de state Jerusalemme die kroote Turke e comsla* (1689).
[4] Ibid., 3.   [5] Ibid.

where the showmen tried to find an audience for their attraction. The difference, however, with watching a firework display is that, although the viewers are part of a broader audience, their 'eye' is 'caught' by the peepshow: it is an eye that is isolated from the collective that surrounds it, suggesting a strange form of intimacy that confronts the viewer with scenes that were not 'intimate' at all, such as the fighting masses on a battlefield and looting soldiers. Consequently, according to Brusati (1995: 169–82), viewers are present and not present; only their 'look' is present in the scene, not their body, which creates a tension between the simultaneous corporeal exclusion from and optical absorption into the world represented therein.

If the remediation of fireworks in the peepshows and the violence they implied were aimed at gaining and shaping people's interest, we now move to situations in which people's interests propelled them to act – and violently so.

Conflicting Interests, Solidarity and Division: Rioting Bodies on the Street

At the end of January 1696, the Amsterdam theatre temporarily closed its doors, and performances were suspended for a week. The theatre archives from those years have not survived, but in all probability that short-lived closure was related to a local explosion of violence that culminated in the 'Aansprekersoproer' (Undertakers' Riot) on 31 January and 1 February 1696 (Figure 15). The theatre was closed, and the public's gaze temporarily turned to another stage, that of the street. On that stage, the main actors were rebels, along with the suppressors of the revolt (the police and the urban militia) and the 'victims', often members of the Amsterdam political elite whose houses were raided. The rebellious population turned against the financial consequences of two tax increases and the appointment of undertakers as holders of public office. There was great fear that the poor in particular would no longer be able to receive a proper burial as a result of the latter measure – one that, moreover, would stimulate favouritism (Dekker, 1979: 37). In particular, the lower classes were rioting on the street, including people from very different backgrounds, with sailors (the main group), simple workers, orphans, peddlers and a single burgher among them (Dekker, 1982: 34). The taxes in question – on marriage and burials – affected everyone, and different groups merged in a joint struggle, a collective manifestation of bodies that positioned themselves against the rulers by violating the elite's private property. The interests of the urban government, which advocated for a rationalisation of the funeral system that would provide the city with more income, encountered the conflicting interests of broad parts of the urban population that benefitted from the cheapest possible funeral.

In the reports from that time, seeing the rioting bodies on the street evoked different reactions among the spectators. These accounts describe the riot as a public event people can look at and comment on from a safe distance, as if they are part of a theatre audience. The audience responses, as represented in handwritten accounts of the riot, vary from disbelief and horror to understanding and solidarity:

> A decent man, seeing this violence, said 'Well, what is going on? Well, how agitated the people are. The burghers ought to prevent such things and mischief.' He was answered by some of the citizens who stood around him, 'What hell! Would we mind that? Those people are good for us. What do we have to do with all that people and that ordinance' etc. (Dekker, 1979: 51)

The onlookers are divided: some support the citizens who are in the militia and trying to stop the riot; others feel attached to the lower classes and have no intention to stop the rebels because 'those people are good for us'. Despite their different interests, the lower classes and the Amsterdam burghers can both be seen as interrelated 'bodies of interests'. The middle class, for instance, is dependent on the lower classes, who work for them, and vice versa: clerks and servants depend on burghers who pay their wages. The bodies of interest that are thus involved with the riot as a public event are at least partially connected with the rioting bodies on the street, judging from the expressions of solidarity from bystanders.

The dominant perception in the reports, however, is based on a clear dividing line between the two groups, condemning the street violence and distinguishing between the 'decent citizens' who are not involved in the riot and the 'rebels' who are violating private property. The figure of the dangerous rebel is set apart by the printmaker Pieter van den Berge, who made two portraits, one of which (Figure 20) is supposedly a sailor from Boston, according to a note on the copy of the print in the Rijksmuseum. The sailor is depicted here with a knife and a ripped-out heart in his hands, which is reminiscent of violent extremes such as the famous lynching of the De Witt brothers in 1672. It also reminds us of exoticising images of extreme violence, such as the depiction of a 'cruel Turk' in de Hooghe's print of the revenge on Sultan Osman II by the rebel Abaza Bada in 1623 (Figure 21). Taking away someone else's money and luxury goods is connected here with an extreme form of physical violence. To avoid any sympathy for the violation of property in times of economic decline and poverty amid the self-enrichment of the elites that violation is presented here on the same level as murder – that is, as an extreme form of violence.

Van den Berge's prints are somewhat exceptional compared to most of the other prints dealing with the Undertakers' Riot, such as the series made by

Figure 20 Pieter van den Berge, *Looter in the Undertakers' Riot in Amsterdam* (1696). Rijksmuseum Amsterdam, RP-P-OB-82.884.

Laurens Scherm. Around 1702, he made engravings of three paradigmatic scenes from the public riot of 1696: the protests on Dam Square, the looting of several canal houses by an angry population and the chasing of the looters by the militia. In these prints, the distanced perception of the riot results in depictions of rioting masses, without any reference to the individual perspective of the rioters. Scherm's print of grouping rioters on Dam Square (Figure 15), for example, shows a mass of people whose faces are hidden behind a maze of hats, (broom)sticks and flags, so that most of the faces are obscured or invisible. The crowd is held together by a sense of outrage, stemming from a shared interest that comes into play here through its emotional effect: the indignation that will be discharged in 'mutiny and plunder'.

The threatening atmosphere of the print emphasises the emotional bonding among the rioting masses, affected by the same feeling, while the subsequent 'mutiny and plundering' resulting from that collective emotion is depicted in another print (Figure 22). In this case, some shocked spectators in the foreground emphasise the aforementioned dichotomy between citizens as

Figure 21 Romeyn de Hooghe, 'Murder of Sultan Osman II by the Rebel Abaza
Bada in 1623', in Hiob Ludolf, *Allgemeine Schau-Bühne der Welt oder:
Beschreibung der vornehmsten Weltgeschichte* [. . .] *Johann David Junner*,
Frankfurt, 1699. Herzog August Bibliothek, Wolfenbüttel, Graph. Res. C: 145.34.

uninvolved spectators and citizens who carry out the act of violence, taking
possession of the private property of one of the mayors: Jacob Boreel.

While the shared interests and the accompanying emotions transform individuals into a mob, these interests potentially connect that mob with uninvolved
bystanders – for instance, with citizens who know that they depend on these
masses themselves ('they do good for us'). This potential solidarity contrasts with
representations that divide the two groups over and over again on the basis of an
emotional regime that puts peace and order first, based on the interests of the
city's ruling classes, while pointing the finger at those who do not adhere to that
regime, causing disorder and violence, carried away as they would be by their
own anger and greed. The contrast present here is typical for early modern
approaches towards the common people as a distinct socio-economic reality on
the one hand, whereas, on the other hand, the category of 'the mob' was not fixed
at all. In fact, the boundaries between, often interdependent, lower and higher
social groups were rather fluid, and social mobility was possible, especially in the
Dutch Republic (Jacob & Secretan, 2013: 2–3; Deursen, 1991: 13–22).

The affective dividing line that was present in the popular imagery charac-
terises the institutionalised representation of the Undertakers' Riot. These

Figure 22 Laurens Scherm, *Riot on the Dam Square and Looting Mob*. Etching.
Rijksmuseum Amsterdam, RP-P-OB-82.872.

official representations further accentuate the dichotomy by referring to the
Amsterdam *burgers* (burghers) as a group with a shared interest that is explicitly
contrasted with that of the mutinous *grauw* (the lower classes). One of the most
telling examples is the commemorative medal that was planned to be minted by
order of the Amsterdam magistrate with the following verse:

> Due to Amstel's wise advice
> And burghers' courage,
> The mutinous mob
> And its malice are subdued.

(Dekker, 1979: 98)

In early modern Dutch, different affects could be related to the emotional concept of *moedwil*, which refers to a *wil* (will) that is not directed by reason but by *moed* – that is, the heart. *Moetwil* or *moedwil* – here translated as 'malice' – sums up all the emotions that would have underpinned the riot: the wilfulness of the population, but also its anger, the vehemence and wantonness of the revolt, the underlying desires, rebellious passions and the lustfulness that is connected with looting.

The coin brings the conflict of interests to a head by fuelling it with emotional connotations that explicitly denounce the rebellious mob. The city council is playing a dangerous game here, as one of the reporters suggests, referring to a critical debate about these verses. Some people thought it would be better to remain silent about the conflict instead of making a coin that would deepen the division within urban society and perpetuate it into 'eternal memory' (Dekker, 1979: 97–8). Perhaps this is why the commemorative medal referring to the 'mutinous mob' was never minted.

The medals that did survive (Figure 23) do not emphasise the dichotomy between the two bodies of interest but refer to an urban community that is held together by the public interest of the commonwealth. This is in line with resolutions and other official documents that often refer to the urban community as a united body of burghers and inhabitants, focussing on a shared urban identity instead of socio-economic differences and political privileges (Boone & Prak, 1995: 116–17).

As the medal shows, the public interest implies not only peace and social tranquillity, captured here by the rising sun, but also an economy that will be able to revive now that calm has returned to the city, and the god of the seas can

Figure 23 Medal commemorating the suppression of the Undertakers' Riot, Amsterdam, 1696. Rijksmuseum Amsterdam, NG-VG-1-1696.

bring back prosperity. The process of calming down is expressed by a turbulent sea on one side and a calm sea on the other. The sea may thus refer to the unstable 'mood' of the Amsterdam population, to the political and social unrest and rest in the city but also to the water as a way to access to trade and welfare.

The population is represented here by a nest with birds, two of which are in danger of falling out of the nest on the stormy side, while on the quiet side they again inhabit the nest in harmony. Peace and harmony here are the result of the efforts of Neptune, who tames the sea, rebukes the maritime winds and restores peace. Neptune is the god of the sea, but also of sea trade, as well as a reference to the good governance of the city council, as his chariot bears the Amsterdam coat of arms. As with the fireworks, the aim of these coins is to construe a feeling of unity and peace in the years following a period of unrest and violence and to steer the interest of the audience away from scenes of conflict towards a prospect of peace and prosperity. In the context of profitable trade, but also with regard to a divine entity that promotes peace and harmony, these two sides of the medal emphasise the importance of the ability to control violence. This will be the main topic of the next section.

4 Control: Unruly Power, Civilising Markets

State Violence: A Market for Violence

The abundant display of violence on a representational level, growing especially in the second half of the seventeenth century, showed a new commercial realm for violent spectacle. Was it then, as the term *spectacle* suggests, something to be simply enjoyed? Or did it (also) have a pedagogical function? Did the excessive display of violence actually propel the desire to restrict and control it? And how did these representations relate to 'real' acts of violence? What is the relation between physical violence and imagined violence?

For more than a century, scholars have been debating the decline of violence in Western civilisation. Seminal studies such as Johan Huizinga's *The Waning of the Middle Ages* (1919), Norbert Elias's *The Civilizing Process* (1939) and Steven Pinker's *The Better Angels of Our Nature* (2011) have described the monopolisation and decline of violence and transitions from cultures of honour and uncontrolled passions where instrumental violence was valorised to cultures of dignity, self-restraint and rationality. Historians have praised, integrated, criticised and nuanced this 'grand narrative' – for instance, by pointing out that non-physical categories of violence, such as assaults on personhood or dignity, should also be taken into account (Broomhall & Finn, 2016; Dwyer & Damousi, 2020; Dwyer & Micale, 2021). In this section, we aim to contribute to the discussion by analysing the dynamics between physical and

Figure 24 Inner square of the 'Rasphuis', the prison for men at Heiligeweg 19, Amsterdam, around 1680. Print by Hugo Allard originally published in Melchior Fokkens, *Beschrijvinge der wijdt-vermaarde koop-stadt Amstelredam* (1662). Amsterdam Archive, 010097000047.

imagined violence, while paying particular attention to the public expression of violent state power.

In the Dutch Republic, historians indeed see a reduction in physical public violence over the course of the early modern period. They have argued that two characteristics of the violent public expression of governmental judicial power – namely, its taking place in public and its use of the physical infliction of pain – disappeared (Spierenburg, 1984; Schama, 1988). The possible reduction of state violence was exemplified, for instance, by the innovative Amsterdam prison system: the 'Rasphuis' for men (Figure 24) and 'Spinhuis' for women. In these institutions, correction or re-education was more prominent than punishment. Thus, the convicts were put to work: to shave wood, in the case of men, or to spin and sew, in the case of women. As if to emphasise the new role of public administration, the Rasphuis was led by a 'father', who was the superior of the 'master of discipline' (Spierenburg, 1991: 108). For sure, conditions were still harsh, and many died in prison. Yet the element of correction showed a restrained or controlled use of state violence. Moreover, the new institution was intrinsically connected to both commercial and educational impulses. The Spinhuis, for instance, was financed by the taxes on alcohol and tobacco (Schama, 1988), while citizens were invited to visit these houses of correction and marvel at how formerly unruly bodies were disciplined into a productive labour force and re-educated to become decent citizens again.

Quite early on, the Dutch elites seem to have become uneasy with the public sight of judicial violence. First, permanent scaffolds were replaced by temporary scaffolds. Then, magistrates slowly started to retreat from their prominent position at executions. In this process, the masses started to be criticised for their supposedly unhealthy interest in violent justice (Spierenburg, 1984: 186; Duijnen, 2019: 119–20). A comparable development can be seen in relation to torture. In the course of the eighteenth century, almost all rulers throughout Europe started to reform a judicial system that was still based on the *Constitutio criminalis Carolina* from 1530, a document that had underpinned many witch trials and torture practices (Emsley, 2007). In the Dutch Republic, this process had already started in the sixteenth century (Nierop, 2009; Gemert, 2008). Throughout Europe, over the course of the seventeenth century, torture was used with more and more restrictions, due to 'the development of new criminal sanctions and the revolution in the law of proof' (Langbein, 1978: 23). Some scholars even described this as a 'dramatic decline' (Silverman, 2010; Paalvast, 2011). Obviously, torture did not disappear, but it disappeared from the public space, and its function changed. Punishment or the extortion of evidence became less paramount than torture's 'powerful cultural significance' (Silverman, 2010: 24).

Simultaneously, the book-and-image market witnessed an explosion of violent imagery, made possible by the technical and commercial powers of the Dutch printing houses. The extensive production of famous printing ateliers, such as those of Romeyn de Hooghe and Jan Luyken, shows an abundance of unrestricted, abhorrent and despicable, but apparently also attractive or enjoyable, violence (Duijnen, 2019). The public eye turned from the live scaffold to the marketable image. This, in our eyes, should not be seen as the marketplace simply stepping in to create a substitute for the real 'theatre of horror'. As historians of emotions, we would stress that the desire for spectacles of horror is not inherent in human nature; it is engineered at different times, through different media. The distancing of real, live violence created the opportunity for imaginary theatres of horror. This was also recognised by the playwright and director Jan Vos, who stated that the exuberant representation of violence was made possible *because* the societal circumstances were now less violent (see Section 2). This was not a straightforward transition.

The tension between the rejection of violence in public spaces and the joy in seeing its representation can be illustrated by one of the many violent prints made by Jan Luyken. It concerns the public execution of James Scott, First

Duke of Monmouth, a print made for the 1698 volume by Lambert van den Bos: *Treur-toonneel der doorluchtige mannen, of Op- en ondergang der grooten* (*Tragedy of Honourable Men, or the Rise and Decline of the Powerful*) (Figure 25). Van Duijnen considered this print in the broader context of the market for execution prints, where religious and secular prints were 'blending together into a broader category of judicial violence' (Duijnen, 2019: 113). The execution of the Duke of Monmouth on Tower Hill in London was notoriously clumsy: reports state that it took the executioner between five and eight blows to decapitate the duke, with the condemned man raising his head reproachfully after the first blow. According to some reports, the head had to be severed with a knife in the end. The print, while perhaps offering the viewer a voyeuristic pleasure in the display of violence, mostly captures the clumsiness, and the consternation it provoked, in detail. The accompanying text mentions rightly that Scott's head was 'very miserably cut off'.

Figure 25 Jan Luyken, 'Execution of James Scott, Duke of Monmouth', in Lambert van den Bos, *Treur-toonneel der doorluchtige mannen, of Op- en ondergang der grooten*, 3 vols., 1698. Rijksmuseum Amsterdam, RP-P-OB-44.637.

Whether it is Monmouth himself showing his pain through a frozen grimace and clenched fists, or the face of the executioner, Jack Ketch, desperately trying to sever the head, or whether it is the faces of the bystanders, they all involve the viewer affectively. Here, the image captures the growing unease that audiences experienced with executions in the flesh or testifies to a more general desire to treat convicted persons with more restraint (or at least more skill). Yet, clearly, the print also offers every possibility of a so-called guilty pleasure. If the audience represented in it may be horrified, the reading audience may equally well be enjoying it (Duijnen, 2020). The affective dynamic is thus hovering between rejection and enjoyment of violence, of evoking empathy to express the necessity to control violence.

Controlling Violence: Divine Sovereignty versus Civic Government

Another example of this emotional tension is a eulogy by the famous Dutch poet Joost van den Vondel: 'De getemde Mars', or 'Mars Tamed' (1647). Since the divine embodiment of war and violence, Mars, is its protagonist, the poem excels in giving detailed descriptions of a violence that is both divine and secular in nature and is both evoked and tamed. The dynamic, again, is determined by the spectacular display of violence on the one hand and on the other hand the question of how excessive violence can be controlled, by what means and by whom.

Negotiations between warring European parties that had fought one another for decades had been going on since 1641 in the German cities of Münster and Osnabrück. On the Dutch side, representatives of the Lords States-General of the United Provinces negotiated with the Spanish in Münster. Their talks had partly been concluded on 8 January 1647, when it was decided that there was to be peace. This is why Vondel could write his poem in the summer of that same year, in the 'Oegst maend' or harvest month, August 1647. The month in which Vondel wrote his poem is qualified explicitly for a reason: there were harvests and fruits to be reaped, in this case the fruits and harvests of peace – the so-called Peace of Westphalia (Duits, 1997). The print shown in Figure 26 visualises this peace allegorically, with all the tools of war lying idly in the foreground, while in heaven, Peace (Pax) and Justice (Justitia) rejoice, and Prudence (Prudentia), Reason (Ratio) and Time (Tempus) reforge the weapons of war into plough-shares – in line with the biblical saying. Violence, meanwhile, works the bellows. The text underneath the print says that if peace is stable, justice rules.

Likewise, Vondel's poem sings the praises of peace. Yet, in his case, it was not some divine or quasi-divine force that was able to stop the violence but the burgomasters of Amsterdam, as the major architects of peace. And, whereas in the print all the violence of the past is in the background, with Peace and Justice

Figure 26 Allegory of the Peace of Münster. The 1577 print was originally intended to glorify the Eternal Edict and was reworked to represent the Peace of Münster (1648). Rijksmuseum Amsterdam, RP-P-OB-68.262.

coming out of the dark receding clouds, a large part of Vondel's text describes massive acts of violence. Rightly so, one could say. From all the wars, civil or otherwise, that raged in and across Europe, the Thirty Years' War between 1618 and 1648 stands out as a particularly gruesome one. The wars did lead to a substantial number of representations in word or image of paradigmatic atrocities, such as the sacking of Magdeburg in 1631 by Johann Tserclaes, Count of Tilly, and his rabble: 30,000 inhabitants were raped, tortured and slaughtered; only 5,000 survived (Outram, 2002: 245–72).

When the fighting finally stopped, many major artists of the time rushed to sing or visualise the praises of the peace and of those who had made it possible. Vondel did have a special position in this collective. He represented the Dutch Republic as a civilising force, albeit with a twist (Geerdink, 2012: 181–6). 'Mars Tamed' explicitly brings in the colour orange, a metonymy for the house of the Dutch stadtholders, Orange-Nassau. In this case, the acting stadtholder was William II, a brazen and ambitious young man. As for the Westphalian peace treaty, William II was straightforwardly opposed to it because it diminished his income and power.

Vondel's poem (analysed by Korsten and McGourty, 2023) consists of three building blocks. The first block, the preface, praises the Amsterdam burgomasters as the true architects of the peace. This is the first block in full:

To our fathers of peace, fathers of the fatherland, the lords burgomasters of Amsterdam.

Now a source of happiness bursts from our veins
By the sound of the silver peace trumpet
On which you tune the world's peace
Oh, true fathers of the peace of Amsterdam.
Your wisdom helped braid the orange ribbons
And cords, that now have tamed the violence,
The bitter war, for so long without rest,
On whose heart no wish of peace could be attached.
Europe, yes the entire globe, the four parts
Of the earth's ball, come rolling towards you, rejoicing,
Because you have stopped the well of civil blood
As you were the first to smother this Hydra of conflict.
Now the citizens in your borough crown you,
Because you willingly forfeit your own interests
And devote your care, your labour and your sweat
To the fatherland and the common wealth.
Ay, stay true to the aim of wars
Which is FREEDOM, your hard-won inheritance,
Providing all with shelter under this custody
Bringing harmony and power to your city.

(Vondel, 1931: 251, lines 1–20)

Apparently, the wisdom of the Amsterdam burgomasters, addressed as the true fathers of the peace and of the fatherland, 'helped braid the orange ribbons and cords' that tamed the violence. Braiding is the opposite here of 'unbridled', an implicit hint at the unbridled ambitions of stadtholder William II, who would come to attack Amsterdam in 1650 in a *coup d'état* that aimed to break the power of Holland. He failed, and Vondel wrote in a poem praising the defensive bulwarks of Amsterdam (*Aen de blockhuizen van Amsterdam*): 'Not nobility but a scoundrel lusts to trample with his hoof the crown of cities.' Apart from this 'scoundrel', Vondel was also aware how much the Republic had needed the stadtholders in its military endeavours. The allegory accepts this, then, but makes clear that the powers of the Oranges, their 'ribbons and cords', should be braided by civil powers to tame war's unruly violence.

The second block then describes how Jupiter is dissatisfied with human beings and sends Mars to punish them as a matter of divine wrath. When Mars is more than willing and capable of performing his task, at some point a horrified Europe comes to complain about what is being done to her. So,

Jupiter calls Mars back. The latter refuses and comes to revolt and fight against Jupiter and the entire circle of gods, a war that Mars appears to win. In this context, the figure of Jupiter provokes reflections on the status of both wrathful divine violence and divine justice. The legitimacy of divine violence fascinated Vondel. Mars's revolt against his father and all the other gods has been read as a parallel to Vondel's play *Lucifer*. The play stages God's major angel revolting because God has made human beings, who appear to be the angels' equals. Vondel's *Lucifer* would be worked out in the coming years, from 1648 to 1654 (Duits, 1997: 186). Indeed, parallels between the figures of Lucifer and the character of Mars have their own logic and suggestive force. Yet they escape the nastier or politically charged question of why a baroque playwright would be so fascinated by subjects rising up against their sovereign lord – especially if this sovereign lord is God who can act at will.

The twist in the text rests in the fact that, once Mars is recalled by Jupiter, Mars revolts because Jupiter sent him out in the first place. This leads to a decisive baroque derailment when the poem exults in describing in detail how the gods come to fight one another. The enthusiasm in a long description of violence is effective in that the text itself almost becomes a wagon without reins. In terms of content, the thing to note is that Mars and his armies are described in terms of human artifice; or it is human weapons and techniques – gunpowder against lightning, blunderbusses against thunder – that empower Mars. In addition, it is Mars's robbing the gods of their weapons that shifts the balance. Finally, the conflict in the heavens is not described in terms of a supreme being who is capable of restoring order but of a political order threatened by someone who will not negotiate and will not accept the rule of law – Mars: 'Then Jupiter saw his rule hang in the balance / And the chances of heaven turning, blow after blow. / His enemy would not listen to entreaty, / Nor would he accept laws from a supreme authority. / What consult, Jupiter? Your court starts to burn' (Vondel, 1931: 255, lines 141–5). This brings us back not only to the brutal reality of the Thirty Years' War but also to a more fundamental reconsideration of the relationship between the state and its theological underpinning regarding the question of whether a political and legal order should have, or could have, its fundament in God (Benjamin, 1996).

If Jupiter is, in accordance with the regular allegorical reading, a metaphor for the Christian God, his sovereignty or supreme rule is questioned. Or, to put it bluntly, he is impotent. This is precisely what opens up the inverted allegory, according to which Mars becomes the leader of human armies and armour that are capable of setting the heavens on fire and defeating the gods. The text is a performing object, consequently, in the sense that it works against itself to allegorically reveal a fundamental contradiction in the political household of

Europe. In general, in the seventeenth century, God politically underpins legal and state sovereignty, as when kings are kings 'by the grace of God'. In this text, however, God is incapable of putting the seal on a just order. This provokes the question: if the seal on a just order cannot be the divine, supreme being, what can be?

The answer is stunningly simple and offered in the third block, when finally, a peace goddess, who allegorically symbolises the Dutch Republic, comes to conquer Mars with her beauty. Stunned by her appearance, Mars drops his weapon; she binds him and restores good order: peace. The message is that a republic can rely on itself as a civil society. All it asks, so the poem suggests in the preface and through the allegory of the simple maiden, is decent adminis-tration: people who give up their own interests for the sake of service to the commonwealth. Giving up one's own self-interest implies self-control. Three major routes can lead to this control: education, theatre and the market.

Controlling Violence: Education and the Theatre

The necessity to regulate violence and the urgency of self-control were explored in the realm of philosophy, where the control of disturbing passions was a dominant topic. With Benedict de Spinoza, the body became central to this debate: a body driven by passions. This is why passions needed to be vectorised, controlled by stronger passions or overcome by stronger insights. Three import-ant tools to establish this control were *education*, by means of expanding knowledge and insight; *theatre*, by means of showing people the proper ways to act; and the civilising force of the *market*. The market suffered, however, from a principal ambiguity. On the one hand, the market was considered a force of temperance and civilisation. On the other hand, it was precisely the market that instigated exuberance, excess and greed. If in Spinoza's ideal commercial society the natural rivalry of individuals was to be dominated or tamed by the integrative forces of the market, this depended in turn on a security and freedom of trade guaranteed by the state: 'Thus the purpose of the state is really freedom' (Spinoza, 1958: 231). When Vico remarked that 'Spinoza speaks of the state as of a society which consists purely of shopkeepers', he suggested that this freedom was predominantly a freedom to realise one's interests by means of trade (Wagener, 1994: 482).

One specific breeding ground for the reflection on *education* as an instrument for the control of passions was the revolutionary Amsterdam Latin School, founded around 1652 by one of the more intriguing characters in the Dutch Republic, Franciscus van den Enden (Mertens, 2012). The school was open to boys and girls and attracted the young Spinoza, among others. Both within the school itself and in its *Nachwuchs*, regulation of the passions was key. Theatre was one of the instruments to achieve this goal; or the theatre as an institution should serve the regulation of the passions. This showed itself later in a group of Amsterdam intellectuals who, in their concern for the well-being of the general populace, considered that the control of violence could be achieved by educational means through one institution only: the theatre. In 1669, as the equivalent of the *Académie francaise*, they founded a society called *Nil Volentibus Arduum* (NVA): 'For those who strive, nothing is too hard.'

The history of this society (Holzhey, 2014; Leemans & Johannes, 2013: 259–77) has been described extensively and often reduced to the context of French Classicism. Yet it can best be defined as a manifestation of the Radical Enlightenment (Israel, 2001): a former pupil of van den Enden, Antonides van der Goes, and friends of Spinoza, such as Lodewijk Meyer and Joannes Bouwmeester, were members of the society. The idea was to civilise people and to let them control their passions so that they could come to a clearer or more enlightened vision of the world and its realities. In this context, the representation of violence was out of the question, precisely because violence tended to sweep people along, or would horrify them, as a result of which they could no longer think straight. Violence, whether real or represented, was at the basis of societal disruption. Accordingly, if the members of NVA considered religious themes or issues of state not adequate for the theatre, this was not to isolate an aesthetic realm but because religion and issues of state tended to arouse the emotions of people too much. Restricted representation of violence was intrinsically connected, in this analysis, to the reduction of real (state) violence.

The trend to control violence led to other outcomes in different realms of the image market. While books and pamphlets were filled with violent images, theatrical societies such as NVA tried to cleanse the stages in the Dutch theatres of violence. Yet this attempt counteracted the transition from a state-informed theatrical regime to a commercially propelled spectacle which embraced the staging of violence to attract the public (see Section 2). The members of NVA constantly had to balance their ideals of 'civilised' theatre with the desires of the public. The Amsterdam theatre therefore hosted a mixture of plays. The playwright Jan Vos, for instance, not only used to stage violent scenes in the theatre but also designed labyrinths, with *tableaux* and statues that could move mechanically (Spies, 2001: 71). Far from providing the visitor with moral lessons, the labyrinth was first and foremost a matter of 'exuberant, at times unchaste, farcical, and comical shows, full of affects and emotions' (Korsten 2017, 194). Still, this was about to change. Towards the end of the seventeenth century, the Amsterdam labyrinths showed a growing control of what was being shown, with religious themes becoming more dominant. This signalled 'a changed cultural interest', with a Republic that tried to become 'decent', even in the garden of statues (Spies 2001: 78). Analogously, in studies on humour and farces, the 'culture of frivolous ambiguities was taken in the stranglehold of moral seriousness' (Stipriaan, 2016: 188).

The general picture is blurred, then. Whereas violence was a problem of collective concern, it had also become a thing that could be sold in a market propelled by desires, fears, indignations or perverse joys. In this context, it is noteworthy that NVA did not include issues of trade in the themes to be avoided. To them, the market could well function as a controlling and civilising mechanism (Johannes & Leemans, 2018). Here, we encounter yet another ambiguity or tension: a tension between the ways in which trade and violence were represented and how they were connected in reality.

Doux commerce? Violence Controlled by Self-Regulating Markets

In the second half of the seventeenth century, the Dutch print market exploded. One example was the print series *Les Indes Orientales et Occidentales*, a publication dominated by representations of diverse, global violence (see Introduction). Still, the engraver Romeyn de Hooghe also treated the viewer to unexpectedly peaceful scenes, such as the market at Bantam (Figure 27).

The print offers an example of a clever engineering of images. The violent and culturally diverse disorder of nature, religion or politics in the other prints is contrasted here with the orderly conduct of the market. De Hooghe portrays commerce ('Koophandel' on the banner above) as both a profitable and a civilising endeavour. Chinese, Javanese and European traders, producers and consumers all come together in peaceful negotiations in an urban environment that has clearly profited from this market economy. Commerce, as the combination of image and heading explain, entails fishery, transportation, bulk trade, merchant negotiations, information exchange and the private consumption of foodstuffs and household items but also regulation: customs, weighing, taxation and surveillance. The latter is present through the watchtower and the castle in the background but also in the left-hand margin, where military personnel watch the entire scene.

The market as a civilising force was a theme to which Romeyn de Hooghe returned. Not only in his prints but also in his textual productions, he praised the stabilising and pacifying qualities of trade and commerce (Daudeij, 2021). Historians, however, usually place the praise of commerce, or the conceptualisation of trade as a positive, profitable, pacifying and stabilising force – the *doux commerce* – later in time: in the Enlightenment, with Montesquieu, David

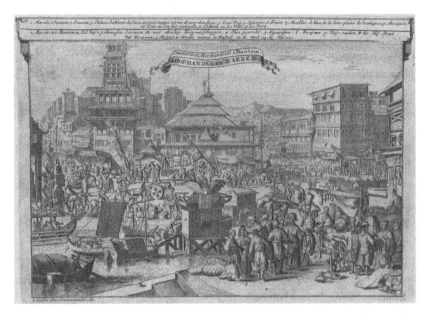

Figure 27 Romeyn de Hooghe, 'Market and trade in Bantam: Commerce et marchandises à Bantam', in *Les Indes Orientales et Occidentales et autres lieux*, etching, 1682; Rijksmuseum Amsterdam, BI-1972-1043-8.

Hume and Adam Smith as the main advocates (Pomeranz & Topik, 1999: 141–70; Terjanian, 2013). Apparently, in the Dutch Republic, the glorification of trade as both a profitable affair and a civilising, stabilising and binding factor for society had a longer tradition. Here, as well, the regulation of passions was a key aspect. Poems, for instance, praised the Dutch regents and merchants for putting their wealth to the greater glory of Dutch society: for 'wresting' the Dutch polders from the sea, investing in urban architecture and donating money to support the poor, orphans or the elderly (Johannes & Leemans, 2018). In this context, investing profit to support the common good helped overcome the religious and moral challenges underlying the accumulation of wealth (Sturkenboom, 2019; Jacob & Secretan, 2008).

The *oeuvre* of Pieter and Johan de la Court, specifically *Interest van Holland, ofte gronden van Hollands-Welvaren* (*Interest of Holland, or the Fundaments of Dutch Well-Being*) (1662), was pivotal in this context. Their work helped develop an ideal of so-called commercial republicanism. With advocates such as the de la Courts, Dutch republicanism moved away from classical republicanism, which regarded trade and luxury as undermining civic virtues. Instead, they proposed commerce as a suitable force to underpin the stability of the state (Weststeijn, 2012). No coincidence, then, that when Amsterdam started working on its new city hall in 1648, the year in which the Peace of Münster was celebrated, it wanted the building to be crowned with a statute of Peace holding an olive branch in one hand and a staff of Mercury in the other.

Yet, in his depictions of the peaceful market scenes, de Hooghe cleverly tries to marginalise the effective and affective control needed for commerce to reach such a quiet state. Commercial markets need the nearly constant affective involvement of their participants (see Sections 2 and 3); therefore, markets need to raise desires and keep people interested. Images played an important role in doing just this. Witness the impressive number of images of the Amsterdam stock exchange that were put on the market in the seventeenth century. From the moment the Amsterdam stock exchange, designed by architect Hendrik de Keyser, opened its doors in 1611, it attracted artistic attention. Poets such as Roeland van Leuve sang the praises of this 'altar of commerce' or 'global castle of trade' (''s Waerelds Koopslot'), while Vondel called it a busy 'beehive' ('Inwydinge van 't Stadthuis t'Amsterdam'). Representations of this international commercial hub became a market in themselves.

Two early prints (Figures 28 and 29) set the tone, depicting the bourse as a majestic building, a space which attracted different groups of people to carry

Figure 28 The Amsterdam stock exchange, c.1612. Printmaker: Claes Jansz Visscher. Publisher: Willem Janszoon Blaeu. Amsterdam Rijksmuseum, RP-P-1880-A-3841.

Figure 29 Inner square of the Amsterdam stock exchange (dated 1609, before the opening of the bourse). Printmaker: Boëtius Adamsz Bolswert. Amsterdam Rijksmuseum, RP-P-OB-67.488.

out commerce. Merchants swarm the bourse floor, male and female citizens are attracted by the shops in the arches and tourists can gaze at the mercantile action from the windows of the first floor of the building, which also offered a shopping mall where one could buy luxury products without the inconvenience of wind or rain. People even walk on the roof.

In one of the various paintings that the artist Jan Berkheyde made of the bourse, there are also young girls selling shiny, fragrant oranges at the gates. The clocks and paintings hanging on the bourse walls were used to attract buyers to the shopping mall. The bourse thus functioned as a clever way to encourage desires (Leemans, 2021a). And the engravings, which were sold in the shops and streets around the stock exchange, helped encourage commercial desires. The connection between the representations of the stock exchange in Figures 28 and 29 with the de Hooghe engravings consists in their depicting the market as a space of wealth, order and civilisation, connecting people from all over the world in peaceful negotiations. And just as with de Hooghe, the bourse print producers seem to suggest that order and stability are inherent or intrinsic to the market.

In these representations, the global context of commerce was not connected to the necessary violence employed to assure the flood of goods streaming into the staple market. Second, although the images did present the bourse as an Amsterdam building, they did not show that the Amsterdam regents had their own office on the first floor of the building, from which they could not only trade but also regulate. In fact, in daily life, the entire bourse was a matter of regulation, since negotiations were allowed only within the bourse and only at certain hours. Within the bourse, moreover, bourse janitors had to maintain law and order. In a rare portrait of one of these (Figure 30), the janitor proudly points at the crowded but orderly bourse floor, indicating that keeping people's passions under control needed a restraining hand. The two dogs at the front of the bourse floor may have been added on purpose. Dogs may sniff in a friendly fashion at one another, but, without a strong hand to keep them under control, they can also become quite unruly.

Still, explicit references to the governance and regulation of the bourse were rare. Stock exchange engravings would certainly insert the coat of arms of

Figure 30 Portrait of Johannes de Paep, janitor (*Beursknecht*) of the Amsterdam stock exchange, standing on a balcony pointing at the crowded but orderly bourse floor (around 1650). Printmaker: Cornelis Visscher. Amsterdam Archive, 010001000053.

Amsterdam, as happens here in Figure 30: the three crosses and two lions in the upper left-hand corner. Yet images of the bourse always concealed the massive city hall that was right behind the bourse building, as if the bourse existed outside the control of the authorities. Finally, a prison called the 'cortegaard' (derived from 'corps de garde') that was installed in one of the corners of the bourse and used by the night watch to lock up drunkards, tramps and misbehaving merchants was depicted only once.

The market of the bourse was thus visualised as a world of decent self-organisation. Or, rather, the violence used by the invested powers to channel the aroused desires of the marketplace was cleverly omitted from the picture. This was so successful that historians have long described the Dutch market as an orderly, open and tolerant space. The general picture is that the prudence of the merchants, combined with the fatherly eye of the regents, who would interfere only in times of crisis, shielded the market from exuberance and violence. Still, by adapting the Enlightenment ideal of *doux commerce* through the idealised representations of the seventeenth century, historians continue to disconnect the history of Dutch and global capitalism from the history of colonial violence. Surely, the explosive distribution of marketable representations of forms of violence fitted paradoxically in a society that had grown less violent *internally*. Yet the Dutch Republic was an extremely violent actor in the international force field of trade. It presented a self-image of being a trading nation, therefore peaceful and non-violent, and when violence was involved, this was always the violence of others. This was a falsehood to which we turn in the next section.

5 Exploitation: The Affects of Empire

The Dutch Republic cherished a picture of itself as a peaceful, tolerant trading society. To safeguard this image, the substantial violence used elsewhere had to be marginalised, silenced, hidden, projected onto others or simply taken as a matter of fact. Still, whereas in some cases the violence used was dealt with in a brutally common-sense kind of way, in others it caused uneasy feelings of guilt. It could even lead to perverse guilty pleasures – or be glorified. The confusing mix of emotions both led to and was propelled by selectively engineering images in such a way that an ambiguous mix of confidence and anxiety was produced or exuberant joy and guilt. The texts and artefacts shamelessly accepted exploitation or were testimony to the suspicion and fear that others (especially the English) would be smarter in getting to the spoils (Onnekink & Rommelsem, 2019: 51–95). This dynamic of hiding and showing was not stable throughout the seventeenth century, and could differ according to the situation, and the fact that violence was hidden may also have been a result of later centuries that wanted to glorify the past under the heading of a 'golden age', a point raised by the anthropologist Michel-Rolph Trouillot in *Silencing the Past: Power and the Production of History* (1996). For those who wanted to see and know, though, there was ample evidence of violence – sometimes depicted in the margins of imageries, sometimes at centre stage.

Framing Violence in the Margins

The 'New Map of the World' shown in Figure 31 was part of just one of the many atlases produced in the Dutch Republic (Schmidt, 2015; Hunt et al., 2010; Groesen, 2008; Dackerman et al., 2011). The margins to the left and the right show different scenes of affective economies that were connected to a local and global force field. The top right-hand corner shows an abundance of profit to be gained by agricultural production and trade. The bottom right-hand corner presents a scene familiar to those living in times of the Little Ice Age, around 1650, when during winters the Low Countries would change into a network of frozen waters that allowed people to stop working and enjoy the art of skating. In contrast, the scenes in the left-hand margin are explicit about what under-pinned all this: the use or control of violence (Figure 32).

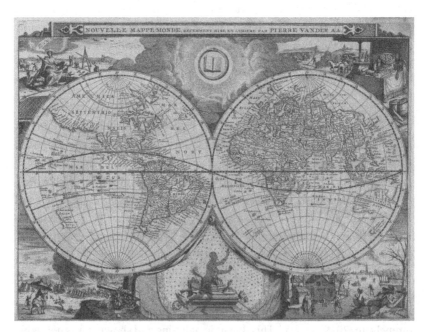

Figure 31 Romeyn de Hooghe, 'New Map of the World', in Pieter van der Aa, *Les Indes Orientales et Occidentales et autres lieux,* Leiden (after 1699). Rijksmuseum Amsterdam, BI-1972-1043-2.

Figure 32 Detail from the lower left-hand corner of the 'New Map of the World' (Figure 31).

In Figure 32, a cannon, with its materiel lying next to it, is blasting out fire and a cloud of smoke. In the background, armies are fighting one another, with casualties scattered in between; a village or city is on fire behind them. Meanwhile, a European military leader, from his elevated vantage point and well protected against an apparently blazing sun, is giving orders. No hints are given as to where the scene is taking place, though the shape of the tents and the parasol suggest it is somewhere in either the Near East or the Far East.

The scene in the upper left-hand corner provides the violence portrayed below with an honourable motivation (Figure 33). Here, farmers are ploughing the soil and sowing, with a shovel and harrow lying ready, while scientists are discussing, studying or measuring the globe and the skies. The foreground presents a woman who emblematically connotes Peace, Justice, Science and Reason. She is partly an indicator of the staple market of knowledge in the Dutch Republic but also a symbol of how violence can be controlled by reason. Owing to the rule of Reason, the drums of war remain silent: a halberd, the now silent cannons and the shield on which the woman's foot rests are lying idle on the ground. The fuse behind her has been extinguished. Still, a single breath would be all it needed to spark again should there be those who would resist the enforced peace.

The fact that the violence is presented in the margins, underpinning the figure of peace or knowledge, and by implication order, allows the viewer a sober realisation that conquering the world is an endeavour with the noble goal of bringing about peace and prosperity through violence. Violence is not shown here to exult in it or be fascinated by it. Nor does its position in the margins

Figure 33 Detail from the upper left-hand corner of the 'New Map of the World'
(Figure 31).

make it a marginal issue. In fact, all the images in the corners function as
a frame. Reading the images symmetrically, in combining left and right, the two
pictures in the upper left- and right-hand corners emphasise the productive
working of the land, of science and of trade. The two pictures below them
show the two faces of playing or gaming, the more frivolous one being skating
and the serious one the 'game of war' (Nelson & Daems, 2019). Taken together,
the images suggest an affective economy, with violence partly being
a disruptive force but also a framing or protective one, suggesting that the
interests at stake can always be defended.

The protective aspect of violence with regard to the Republic's interests is
emphasised in an expansive poem from 1671, in four books, by Antonides van
der Goes called *De Ystroom* (*The River IJ*). The poem defined the Amsterdam
IJ – partly river, partly sea arm – as a rivulet or a stream, indicating that its
waters were an extension of a stream that connected Amsterdam with the global
seas. With the protagonist sailing those seas, the poem offers a poetic equivalent
to the travelling stories that were massively popular in the Republic. In many of
these stories, extreme, exotic violence would be centre stage (Schmidt, 2015:
163–226). Being exotic, this violence would almost always be the violence of
others. If it concerned Dutch violence, it would be justified as a necessary
matter, or a matter of reason. This is, for instance, how the fictive traveller
describes Dutch violence when he has entered the regions of the East Indies:

> From here, either equipped for commerce or war
> We thunder upon all Indian coasts on both sides
> And hold the power in the balance of a hundred princes
> And kings, so that no warrior out of boundaries

(just like an elephant ruminating its old grudge
In the end will break and shatter its iron cage
Throwing trees with its trunk from the soil with root and all
Pulverising his own driver or whatever stops him to mortar)
Comes to revolt, suppressing his neighbours with pride,
And placing Batavia in his shadow with his fortune.
Whereas the Company, through its strong and useful tools,
Keeps them in check, the sword of war bound in its sheath,
Knowing like a state's doctor who reads the signs what spirit
runs through the empire's pulse, they all obediently follow her discipline.

(Van der Goes, 1671, Book 2: 43–4)

Dutch violence is made explicit: 'We thunder upon all Indian coasts'. It is defined as a reasonable violence against those who step out of bounds, metaphorised in the elephant gone berserk – and the elephant is a common emblem for Asia (Schmidt, 2015: 233–5). The East India Company – or VOC – is a containing, regulating, reasonable, disciplining ruler, then, who knows how to keep madness in check. This was a far cry from the company's real behaviour, yet the depiction of its violence as a necessary tool of discipline in the name of peace, justice and order was productive in its dialectical relation with the unchecked violence exercised by 'others'. The difference, affectively speaking, was one between an actor who was able to control themselves and someone who could not.

This 'other' was not necessarily exotic; it could also be European, as when the poor Dutch had been suffering the violence of the Spanish, Habsburg empire. Probably one of the most ironic passages in van der Goes's poem concerns a meeting between Dutch sailors travelling the globe and the ghost of the last Inca emperor, 'Atabaliba' – a European version of the name Atahualpa. His suffering and moaning ghost still wanders along the shores of Panama, where he meets the travelling Dutchmen, who are consequently considered to have suffered the same fate, due to Spanish rule:

[…] Oh, he said, you who like me
Has felt the strikes of Spanish tyranny
Do not be bored to hear about my disaster and misfortune
As soon as the new fleet entered this strip
By landing in Panama (wish it had never landed,
And why did I not put it on fire immediately).
There was this rumour in court: in floating palaces
A bearded species came travelling from another world
Not black, but with a face as white as chalk.
A cold fright races through my members, the head faints
A painful premonition; I feel my throne crack thrice
A fearful and deep sigh rolls three times over the roofs

Of the court, and had fate not betrayed me then
The palace of Magokappe and Kusko would still be standing.
I'd have slaughtered them on the beaches, conquered the weak fleet
And would have shed their godless blood with joy.
Yet there they come; and with eagles' eyes look
For gold, their highest good and only sanctity
They devour it like hungry ravens
Going for the bait; you see them running everywhere
And grabbing; one ships follows after another now.
This is when the entire realm starts to shout blue murder
Who could oppose them? They fire and thunder
As if the abyss came storming upon us from below
And earth and heaven, overpowered by their bullying,
Had sworn in on their faithless, cursed bond.
What madness did you bring, say, bloody tyrants,
Banned so far from our skies and lands
To raid our property, and the empire, where not one foot
Could place itself with right, manuring it with our blood.

(Van der Goes, 1671, Book 2: 40–1)

The Spanish fury is once more depicted here in detail: the poem serves to show how the Spanish behaved like slaughtering brutes in the Americas, in much the same way as they had behaved in the Low Countries.

Horror in Bookkeeping: Data Processing

In his abundant description of Spanish violence against innocent peoples, van der Goes might feel relieved not to have to describe how the Dutch behaved towards the Indigenous peoples of the Moluccas, especially on the Banda Islands, or towards the Africans whom they enslaved and brought to Brazil, or towards the Indigenous peoples living in the Americas, north and south. The resulting discrepancies were described by the historian Judith Pollmann as follows:

> While supporters of the West India Company continued to fantasize about the possibility of natural alliances between the Dutch and the 'Indian' victims of Spanish tyranny, Dutch settlers waged war against native Americans. And while the extermination of virtually the entire population of the Banda islands, in 1621, attracted criticism within Dutch East India Company (VOC) circles, it was only the first of a long range of vicious campaigns against Asian enemies, in which civilians were not spared.   (Pollmann, 2018: 103)

The brutal reality of what was going on was not unknown then. By 1886, a full picture of what had happened in the Dutch Indies could be known by a general populace (Chijs, 1886). Still, that it *could* be known did not mean that it *was* known. The violence used was often a matter kept safely and silently in the archives of the VOC, a 'data-processing organisation' that needed all information (Pollmann, 2018: 103), whether it concerned the Atlantic slave trade or the perhaps even more substantial Indian Ocean slave trade (Baay, 2015; Rossum, 2015; Harms et al., 2013; Stanziani, 2020).

One particular instance of detailed information concerns the Governor-General of the Dutch Indies in 1618–23 and 1627–9: Jan Pieterszoon Coen. At some point, he disagreed wholeheartedly with the treaty that the 'Heeren XVII', the members of the board of the VOC, had concluded with the English East India Company (Widjojo, 2009). In the mind of the VOC lords, agreeing to disagree was better than trying to chase the English out and risk endless acts of retaliation. It brought Coen to commit an act of calculated appropriation: in 1621, he took the Banda Islands, part of the Moluccas, to make it impossible for them to trade with the English. His troops killed the inhabitants, an estimated 15,000 people, and Coen replaced them with a slave workforce acquired from neighbouring regions under the supervision of Dutch 'perkeniers', or 'gardeners' (Loth, 1995). On every step of his actions, Coen reported to the lords of the VOC, sometimes in detail.

The mindset shown by Coen in his reports had already been apparent when in 1611–12 the Dutch explorer Hendrik Brouwer – later a member of the VOC board and Governor-General of the East Indies between 1632 and 1636 – reported that one could deal with the Indigenous people at will: 'One should not ponder too much that this will raise concerns, because they are only blacks and naked people' (Romein & Verschoor, 1977: 274). Affectively speaking, one could define this as a matter of indifference. There were others, though, who did care and reported on Coen's atrocities. The eyewitness Nicolaes van Waert described in detail what happened to forty-four Indigenous leaders who had been taken prisoner and executed without due process:

> [. . .] 6 Japanese with their sharp cutting swords cut the 8 leaders though the mid-section, then cut their heads off and the rest in four parts; the other 36 got their heads cut off and were cut in four parts like the first; an execution that was so cruel it was hard to watch. They all died in utter silence without making any mischief; although there was one who asked in our Dutch language: 'My lords, is there no mercy, then?' But it was to no avail.
>
> (Colenbrander, 1934: 242)

The phrase that it was 'so cruel it was hard to watch' connotes disgust, indignation, empathy and compassion. A prominent merchant who had returned to the Netherlands, Aert Gysels, showed sympathy in considering the execution disproportionate, since it concerned people who had fought for their freedom, just as the Dutch themselves had done. Moreover, the lords of the VOC reported back to Coen: 'This will breed awe, though not favour' ('t Sal wel ontsagh, maer geen gunst baeren'). In this case, the affective response was one of worry and unease.

All this concerned communication in letters and reports or in secret commissions; the general audience would learn only bits and pieces about what had taken place. It was the task of artistic representation to keep intact the general picture of the Dutch as a peace-loving nation; or, not to leave it intact but to produce images in which any kind of violence was projected onto exotic others, as part of a profitable market that served the lust for sensation, or *not* to represent it (Schmidt, 2015: 163–226; Sint Nicolaas & Smeulders, 2021). The prints shown in *East- and West Indian Mirror* (*Oost ende West-Indische Spiegel*) (Figure 34) are an example of such non-representation. They show two islands in the Moluccas: Ambon and Banda Neira.

In Figure 34, trading ships lie near the coast, waiting for supplies and goods. There are a few houses and villages, the suggestion of vegetation and woods and fortresses that symbolise defence and protection. Obviously, the fortresses are also tools of oppression, and especially in the lower image there is perhaps little

Figure 34 View of Ambon and Banda Neira; Anonymous (engraver/etcher), Jan Jansz (publisher), c.1621. Printed in Joris van Spilbergen, *Oost ende West-Indische spiegel der 2 leste navigatiën* [. . .] (1646). Rijksmuseum Amsterdam, RP-P-OB-75.475.

vegetation because it had consciously been destroyed (on which more in the next section) between 1609 and 1621. As for the Indigenous people, they are absent. The one European trader is accompanied by a foreign or Indigenous warrior, apparently in the service of the trader – much as when the Dutch used Japanese executioners to do their dirty work. In this case, the only violence explicitly present is natural, in the shape of an erupting volcano (now called Gunung Api). There is simply no suggestion of what happened to the environment or the peoples of the islands.

Organised Obliviousness: Ecocide

What the Dutch did to the ecology of the Moluccas in the East Indies has been described in terms of an 'extirpation' (Buijze, 2006: 51), or as the removal of a body part. Translated to an ecological context, it means the removal of something that is essentially part of an ecological 'body'. A more brutal term would be 'destruction'. In the case of the Moluccas, the destruction was motivated by one thing: the desire to establish a commercial monopoly. The ecological destruction carried out in the Moluccas by the Dutch in the seventeenth century was a means to establish a monopoly in the trade of mace, nutmeg, sago or cloves and to chase first the Portuguese and then the English out. The destruction of ecological structures was motivated and suggested by the already mentioned Hendrik Brouwer during his travels through the region in 1611–12: 'Now that we know that the Bandanese have no other income than their abundant mass of nut trees [. . .] my advice is [. . .] that one wage war against them with [. . .] the destruction of nut trees [. . .] which can be done more easily and with less peril than conquering their boroughs' (Romein & Verschoor, 1977: 274). When Georg Everhard Rumphius, who would become the greatest European biologist of his time, arrived in Ambon in 1654, he witnessed the reality of what Brouwer had envisaged. For the sake of acquiring a monopoly, Adriaan de Vlaming van Oudshoorn, Admiral of Ambon, Banda and Ternate, had set out on the complete destruction of sago palms on those islands not falling under the supervision of the VOC.

In a manuscript that offered a full description of Ambon's natural environment, Rumphius reports that this had led to a deeply felt hatred on the part of the Indigenous peoples, who had lost the trees on which they were dependent:

> [A]s experience has repeatedly taught, there is no better way of securing the everlasting grudge of people than to cut their fruit and spice trees, and one should not proceed to do so unless one has every reason to destroy the entire nation, then, as Admiral de Vlaming in his latest wars has proven with the total extermination of these lands. (Buijze, 2006: 52)

If this had been a tactic, the results could have been temporary. Yet, as Rumphius reports later, the destruction had lasting impacts, in part due to the stupidity of those in charge, who thought they could simply replant and pick the fruits or spices shortly after:

> Likewise, Commander Frans Leendertsz Valk, with eight companies of soldiers, 150 sailors and 200 blacks, was sent to the clove woods of Mamala and Caphala, from which supplies came to the Wawani on a daily basis, taking no more than two days to destroy all the beautiful clove and coconut trees, as if the Company wanted to abandon these shores for good. Apparently, ignorance dominated the minds of our lords in thinking that after 7 or 8 years one could win back fruit-bearing clove trees. (Buijze, 2006: 53)

The large-scale effects of the colonial endeavour in the course of centuries to come have been extensively studied since the 1970s (Bonneuil & Fressoz, 2016). For now, the question is how this ecological destruction was felt or not felt, as part of affective economies at work, in the Republic.

If seventeenth-century citizens witnessed the establishment of what has recently been defined as the 'plantationocene' (Haraway et al., 2016), they were directly or indirectly, explicitly or implicitly, very affectively involved with the violence used to make this happen. Affectively speaking, the technologies used to make the ecological restructuring possible were depicted as purely instrumental, as shown in the image in Figure 35. This image shows how sugar, or 'the white gold', is made from sugar cane. As one can see, there are no Africans laboriously handling the machines and boiling pots in the newly conquered lands of Brazil. The plate was part of a book called *Nova Reperta – New Inventions*. In the background of the image, one specimen of the plantationocene is shown: a vast field of sugar cane that takes up the entire horizon because it has replaced a diverse environment. Still, the new inventions presented by the book made Katharine Park and Lorraine Daston describe the atmosphere as one of a new age, or *aetas nova* (Park & Daston, 2016: 1). This so-called new age consisted in a general affective economy that ruled the times, or rather the times of the wealthier parts of Europe. This affective economy could be so exciting because of organised forms of obliviousness. One paradigm of this obliviousness concerned the slave trade and slave labour.

Silent Horror, Brutal Violence: The Slave Trade and Slave Labour

Between 1638 and 1643, the geographer and astronomer Georg Markgraf was on an expedition to chart the north-eastern coast of Brazil, which at the time was occupied by Dutch forces under Johan Maurits. The chart would be printed as a wall map in several formats, first by Blaeu in 1647 and later by Huych Allard,

Qua Saccharum paretur arte, plurimis   SACCHARVM.   'Pictura, quam vides, docebit te modis.

Figure 35 Jan Collaert I, 'Invention of Sugar Refining (Saccharum)',
engraving, in *Nova Reperta – New Inventions*, after Jan van der Straet (Haarlem,
Philips Galle, 1584; reprint around 1600). Rijksmuseum Amsterdam,
RP-P-BI-6096.

Clement de Jonghe and Pieter Mortier (Storms, 2011: 43). Geographically speaking, the map was impressively accurate. It was also enriched by a number of pictures, most likely made by Frans Post (Storms, 2011: 43). A scene with a sugar mill that was depicted separately on the map by Blaeu (see the Introduction) was repeated here but with other scenes added (Figure 36).

The added scenes had some anthropological value, showing scenes of everyday life or hunting but also of war. One violent element remained absent, though, in the scenes depicted: the capture, trading and exploitation of African people made slaves. With respect to this, Susie Protschky criticised scholars for 'minimizing the despotic traits' of Johan Maurits (Protschky, 2011: 160). As governor of the WIC, he was responsible for the development of the large-scale transatlantic slave trade by the Dutch (Emmer, 2005), the impact of which has been the topic of fierce debates in recent years (Fatah-Black & Rossum, 2016: 28). By not showing this kind of violence, the map is an example of what Gayatri Chakavorty Spivak (1988) called 'epistemic violence'. This is a phrase derived from the Foucauldian notion of *episteme* as a historical dominant that produces kinds of knowledge that define a period with its systems of power and that allow some subjects a voice while

Figure 36 Georg Markgraf, detail from 'Map of the Coast of Pernambuca'. Clement de Jonghe. Maritime Museum Rotterdam, WAE598.

denying one to others. The denial of voice could also be the result of brute violence, as is shown in an almost forgotten but recently often reproduced image by Zacharias Wagener entitled 'Pernambuco Slave Market' (Dresden, Kupferstich-Kabinett, Staatliche Kunstsammlungen, Ca 226/106). The silence embodied in a mass of enslaved people at the back of this painting from around 1641 is an example of 'thick silence' (Korsten & van Dijk, 2020) – the result of a violent threat that is not directly enacted but just around the corner. Several organisations and actors connected to the Dutch Republic had their fair share in producing such forms of silence.

In the decades to follow, the explicit depiction of violence would become less controversial, especially with regard to Surinam. For instance, the military officer and cartographer Alexander de Lavaux was commissioned by the Surinam governor and the directors of the so-called Surinam Society to produce the first map of Surinam (Figure 37). The map showed all the plantations and their owners, as well as a couple of burning villages of so-called marrons, former slaves who had fled and started their own lives. Thus, it gave evidence as to what might happen if one tried to rise up against, or flee, the possessors and appropriators (Sint Nicolaas & Smeulders, 2021: 201–7).

The map offers a detailed representation of violence, though not in the dry form of reports to the VOC or WIC. The silk map is as informative about the

Figure 37 Alexander de Lavaux, detail from 'Map of Surinam,' with a depiction of the plantations and the military action undertaken against the enslaved (1737). Rijksmuseum Amsterdam, NG-539.

land and its inhabitants as it is about the brutal violence with which both are controlled. De Lavaux's visualisation is from the mid-eighteenth century, when the Dutch Republic was losing its dominant position and the vicious toll of the colonial enterprise had already become more and more palpable. The atmosphere is decisively different from the seventeenth century, when the Republic, almost overnight, turned into a global, imperial power, and the use of legitimate and less legitimate violence by the Dutch was something either to be hidden or to be glorified.

Violence Glorified: From Freedom Fighters to Imperial Might

Sea battles gave ample occasion for glorification. At the beginning of the revolt against Philip II, in the 1570s, sea battles were depicted in lavish and expensive tapestries – a more impressive form of art at the time than paintings – such as the ones ordered by the States of Zeeland between 1593 and 1604. In this case, they were not simply glorifying victory though. They were designed by Hendrick Vroom, who had done research into the matter by interviewing eyewitnesses. As a result, they exhibited a distinct realism. This made them even more politically powerful and more popular.

A tapestry depicting the Battle of Veere (Figure 38) presents an overview of a naval battle, with Veere in the upper left background. In the foreground, it shows gruesome details of ships engaged in close combat and sailors drowning. What the tapestries did not show was the violence that took place when the city was conquered or the violent destruction of statues and images that followed. Rather, the gruesome mess of naval warfare is framed by an elaborate set of images above and below, showing the abundance of land and sea, with magical creatures and Lady Peace carrying all the weapons that no longer need to be used. Thus, the frame acts as a reassuring anticipation of the banquets that will follow victory and the freedom related to it. All those miserable souls who were either blown to pieces, drowned or had to live the rest of their lives severely handicapped or gruesomely disfigured are literally and figuratively not in the picture. Because of this, there can be joy in violence. Accordingly, the violence is not regretted but celebrated by means of these tapestries.

Figure 38 The Conquest of Veere (6–18 May 1572); designer: Hendrick Vroom; tapestry weaver: Hendrik de Maecht (c.1599–1603). Zeeuws Museum, collection Province of Zeeland. Photographer: Ivo Wennekes.

Within less than thirty years after the 1580s, when the Low Countries had almost been defeated by the Spanish, what had then become the Dutch Republic had turned global. Half a century later again, in the 1650s, the new Admiralty was built next to the river IJ, and poets such as Antonides van der Goes and Joost van den Vondel sang its praises (see Section 1). In the celebratory poem by Vondel, he addresses the members of the Admiralty as follows:

> Ye Lords, in whose hands the care for the sea traffic is laid
> And who not from hidden corners or far away caverns
> Pressured by misery, need to collect the ships' riggings
> But rest on your warehouse's ready supplies
> More reassured than before, ready to man fleet after fleet
> To the advantage of merchant cities, and the fright of sea tyrants,
> Who under a veil of legality, now provocatively
> Carry their flag, and build their hopes of gaining spoils
> On your patience and inclination to solve conflict
> By reason rather than the sword to make right right;
> Ye Councils, taking your decisions in the water-room
> And under the highest authority of the liberated country
> Safeguarding the lustre and brilliance of the Seven Provinces
> That rest assured through your vigilance, next to God;
> Allow me to call the clarion for this sea's war horse
> Now that the art of building led it to the shores of the ship-filled Y
> So that, when Triton comes to raise his plunder horn,
> He can break through water storms and ship arrays
> Snorting over the surface, kicking and trampling
> The sea pest of the State and its freeborn cities.
>
> (Vondel, 1935: 654–5, lines 1–20)

As becomes clear at the end of this quote, the new building is compared to a war horse that is led to the water and answers the sea god Triton's calls for war. Triton's plunder horn is the response to a 'sea pest', a little earlier defined as those who capture Dutch ships under the veil of charters: privateers, especially English ones. The Admiralty functions next to God here in its defence of a country that managed to free itself and now consists of merchant cities: free cities in free states. In its defence, the Admiralty does not wish to use violence. It would rather solve problems through negotiation and law. Yet the building shows, and ensures, the Dutch can use violence immediately, if necessary. In the name of justice, it can easily swap Lady Justice's balance, as a symbol of reasonableness, for the use of that Lady's sword. Affectively speaking, the poem illustrates the coinciding of a desire for peace and justice and the aggressive quest for profit.

The Maritime Warehouse was built in response to the first Anglo-Dutch war (May 1652 to May 1654). The war exhausted both countries but had a considerable impact on the Dutch, who had imagined themselves rulers of the waves with the world's largest trading fleet at the time. The history of this first war is referred to later in the poem when Vondel describes in detail how 'the bloodthirsty English mad dog came to attack' (line 81). Only a decade after the Maritime Warehouse was finished, it would prove valuable when the second Anglo-Dutch war erupted, from March 1665 to July 1667. This time, fortune was on the Dutch side, as evidenced in a triumphal song that Vondel wrote for Holland's greatest admiral, Michiel de Ruyter, on his victory in the Four Days' Battle (11–14 June 1666).

Vondel frames the real event with a choir of mermaids and mermen and the god Mars descending from the heavens to designate the winner. Yet the battle is presented as a brilliant composition from de Ruyter's hand, supported by the hand of God:

> Where did ever a 'ruiter' carry so honestly
> In his shield the noblest weapon,
> Foresight and war strategy,
> The eye in one hand from above,
> In the middle of that glowing oven,
> Strengthened by God's almightiness.
> This sea hero gave measure and rules
> To so many voices of trumpets,
> Kartaws and blunderbusses, together,
> Like the well-composed art of song,
> And rolled on shorter and longer notes,
> The sound of war over the waters.
> Mermaids and mermen's Triton's horn
> The bass and soprano voice of choirs
> Of Mars, high up in the mast,
> Who came down with the king's flag,
> Rejoicing, in the sea chorales,
> In the wooden and iron grinding of battle
> And contingencies of war.
> Now the old harnass-dances remain silent.
>
> (Vondel, 1937: 212–13, lines 101–20)

The first line makes a pun on 'ruiter', Michaël de Ruyter's family name, which also means 'knight' in Dutch. This 'knight' is conducting an orchestra of war, and Vondel symbolically shifts the sound of war by turning it into triumphant music of victory. Make no mistake, in other poems, Vondel was extremely capable of describing the filth, confusion, pain and horrors of the mess of war, here captured only by the phrase 'the wooden and iron grinding of battle'. Rather, just as was the case with the tapestries, the victorious result of battles appears to have made up for all of war's misery. Violence has come to sound like music to the ears – an aspect of violence that is equally important in terms of affects and emotions.

Whereas, according to Trouillot, since the nineteenth century Western historiographers have silenced nasty or unwelcome parts of the past with hindsight, both the texts and the images in this Element demonstrate the ability of seventeenth-century powers to represent current affairs selectively. Or, if the marketing of violence had enormous potential to take people up in a swirl or spectacle of images, it had equal potential to ensure that in this swirl some things that would spoil the spectacle were not represented or shown.

Conclusion: The Violence of Markets

In this Element, we have described how, in the early modern Dutch Republic, an affective economy of violence developed through the circulation of images. While public violence was becoming more controlled, for instance with fewer public executions, the realm of cultural representation was increasingly filled with violent imagery: from prints, atlases and paintings, through theatres and public spectacles, to peepshows. Although these visual and theatrical domains in which violence was represented could be very different in nature, they had at least two basic characteristics in common. As representations of violence, they not only enabled audiences to *imagine violence*; they also *produced emotions* that *did* things to people.

The recurrent representation of violence marketed a wide range of emotions, from joy, awe, wonder and desire to anger, horror and disgust. These emotions not only entailed strong personal feelings and anxieties but could also function as a binding force, aligning individuals with communities – bodily spaces with social spaces. Although the consumption of images and performances could be a truly private experience, the desires and interests aroused in the representation of violence were also truly social in nature. Not only were the emotions often experienced in public (theatrical) contexts, where people of different groups were brought together, but the individual experience of consuming imagery was also bound to an awareness of bodies in relation to an awareness of collective interests, whether political, religious or commercial.

We could, of course, have chosen other lenses than violence through which to analyse the mutations of the early modern affective economy, such as, for example, honour, happiness or prudence. The representation of violence, however, offers an interesting case in point, as it allows us to analyse the evolution of techniques that were operative throughout the early modern period and to trace how a rapidly expanding commercial visual culture enabled more sustained, 'deep' experiences of emotions. Indeed, the increasingly market-driven, spectacular culture of violence invited spectators to immerse themselves more deeply in the experience – increasing confusion between lived emotions and emotions as representations.

Our Element retraces this development of a culture of spectacle, an emotional regime aiming at immersive experiences, permanently 'tickling' cultural consumers and inviting spectators to 'lose' control, to indulge in emotions. However, we also signalled a growing importance of control (Section 4), where the viewer's affects were steered to less disruptive emotional states, such as the peaceful feelings of unity that fireworks were intended to produce. The techniques of engineering imagery contributed to stabilising a new civic identity, implying a more restrained performance of emotions through a process of permanent reiteration, allowing the individual to perceive him- or herself as both a citizen and a consumer. The consumption of violent imagery thus connects with what Monique Scheer called a mobilising emotional practice: strengthening emotions already there, evoking emotions where there are none and changing or even removing emotions (Scheer, 2012: 209).

This Element intended to present a model for studying early modern visual culture in general and offered some overarching thoughts about the interrelation between images, emotions and markets. Yet our case study, the Dutch Republic, urges more specific conclusions. We have described how, during the seventeenth century, the Dutch Republic experienced an explosion in the market of violent imagery. This 'staple market' of images, by means of its quantity and power to remediate ideas and emotions in shifting places, worked itself loose from control by one specific authoritative body, be it the state, the church or the author. Consequently, the concept of emotional self-control became popular, especially when it concerned people's abilities to cope with extreme passions. The issue was: how to control these passions when the impulses for their arousal only increased with the expansion of consumer culture? It might seem paradoxical that the very market that produced the violent imagery, and the emotions it aroused, also came to be considered part of the solution. But this is indeed what happened. Dutch authors and artists systematically presented 'the market' as a *doux commerce*, a peace-bringing, civilising force. Or they highlighted interest, not so much rational self-interest but invested, social interest, as a force that could secure harmonious coexistence.

Throughout this Element, we have argued that this idealised image of a market bringing peace and harmony went hand in hand with a market that actually not only produced violent imagery but was also extremely violent itself, especially in the Dutch colonies. The colonial exploitation of the Dutch empire was furthered by an image market that marketed a strong image of the Dutch being both powerful and yet not violent in nature. Violence was pushed to the margins of maps, projected onto other cultures, depicted as a force of nature or projected back in time as something that happened in a less civilised past. The best trick the 'devils' of the Dutch creative industries thus played was investing citizens in the recurrent consumption of violent imagery while, on the other hand, pretending that the market was not a violent place. This technique of the artful engineering of imageries has not yet gone out of fashion in our contemporary situation.

References

Abbott, Elizabeth (2010). *Sugar: A Bittersweet History*. London: Duckworth Overlook.

Ahmed, Sara (2004a). *The Cultural Politics of Emotion*. Edinburgh: Edinburgh University Press.

Ahmed, Sara (2004b). Affective Economies. *Social Text* 79 (22), 117–39.

Akerlof, George A. & Shiller, Robert J. (2009). *Animal Spirits: How Human Psychology Drives the Economy, and Why It Matters for Global Capitalism*. Princeton, NJ: Princeton University Press.

Albach, Ben (1977a). De Amsterdamse geschreven bronnen van de Nederlandse theatergeschiedenis. *Scenarium* 1, 92–113.

Albach, Ben (1977b). *Langs kermissen en hoven*. Zutphen: Walburg Pers.

Alcoa Corporation (1942). The Place They Do Imagineering. *Time Magazine*, February 16, 56.

Amir, Ton (1996). De opening van de verbouwde schouwburg te Amsterdam. In Rob Erenstein, ed., *Een theatergeschiedenis der Nederlanden*. Amsterdam: Amsterdam University Press, pp. 258–65.

Baay, Reggie (2015). *Daar werd wat gruwelijks verricht: Slavernij in Nederlands-Indië*. Amsterdam: Atheneum-Polak & Van Gennep.

Bailey, Merridee L. (2017). Economic Records: Sources and Methodologies for Early Modern Emotions. In Susan Broomhall, ed., *Early Modern Emotions: An Introduction*. London: Routledge, pp. 108–12.

Balzer, Richard (1998). *Peepshows: A Visual History*. New York: Harry N. Abrams.

Baudartius, W. (1610). *Morghen-wecker der vrye Nederlantsche Provintien*. Danswick: Crijn Vermeulen de Jonge.

Benjamin, Walter (1996). Critique of Violence. In Michael W. Jennings, ed., *Walter Benjamin: Selected Writings*. Cambridge, MA: Harvard University Press, pp. 236–53.

Best, Shaun (2010). *Leisure Studies: Themes and Perspectives*. London: Sage.

Blom, Frans (2021). *Podium van Europa: Creativiteit en ondernemen in de Amsterdamse Schouwburg van de zeventiende eeuw*. Amsterdam: Querido.

Blom, Frans & Marion, Olga van (2021). *Spaans toneel voor Nederlands publiek*. Hilversum: Verloren.

Boddice, Rob (2017). *The History of Emotions*. Manchester: Manchester University Press.

Bok, Marten Jan (1994). *Vraag en aanbod op de Nederlandse kunstmarkt 1580–1700*. Utrecht: Utrecht University Press.

Bolter, Jay David & Grusin, Richard (2000). *Remediation: Understanding New Media*. Cambridge, MA: MIT Press.

Bonneuil, Christophe & Fressoz, Jean-Baptiste (2016). *The Shock of the Anthropocene: The Earth, History and Us*. New York: Verso Books.

Boone, Marc & Prak, Maarten (1995). Rulers, Patricians and Burghers: The Great and the Little Traditions of Urban Revolt in the Low Countries. In Karel Davids and Jan Lucassen, eds., *A Miracle Mirrored: The Dutch Republic in European Perspective*. Cambridge: Cambridge University Press, pp. 99–134.

Bosch, Lambert van den (1698). *Treurtoonneel der doorluchtige mannen, of op- en ondergang der grooten* [...]. Vol. 3. Amsterdam: Jan Claesz. ten Hoorn.

Bouteille-Meister, Charlotte & Aukrust, Kjerstin (2010). *Corps sanglants, souffrants et macabres: XVIe–XVIIe siècle*. Paris: Presses Sorbonne Nouvelle.

Broomhall, Susan, ed. (2016). *Early Modern Emotions: An Introduction*. London: Routledge.

Broomhall, Susan & Finn, Sarah, eds. (2016). *Violence and Emotions in Early Modern Europe*. London: Routledge.

Brusati, Celeste (1995). *Artifice and Illusion: The Art and Writing of Samuel van Hoogstraten*. Chicago, IL: University of Chicago Press.

Bruyn, Yannice De (2021). Staging Siege: Imagineering Violence in the Dutch Theatre, 1645–1686. PhD thesis, Free University of Brussels / Ghent University.

Buijze, Wim (2006). *Leven en werk van Georg Everhard Rumphius (1627–1702): Een natuurhistoricus in dienst van de VOC*. Den Haag: Buijze.

Burke, Edmund (1757). *A Philosophical Enquiry into the Origin of Our Ideas of the Sublime and Beautiful*. London: printed for J. Dodsley.

Burke, Peter (2016). *What Is the History of Knowledge?* Malden, MA: Polity Press.

Bury, Michael (2001). *The Print in Italy, 1550–1620*. London: British Museum.

Bussels, Stijn, Eck, Caroline van & Oostveldt, Bram Van, eds. (2021). *The Amsterdam Town Hall in Words and Images: Constructing Wonders*. London: Bloomsbury.

Casey, Emma & Taylor, Yvette, eds. (2015). *Intimacies, Critical Consumption and Diverse Economies*. London: Palgrave Macmillan.

Chijs, Jacobus A. van der (1886). *De vestiging van het Nederlandsche gezag over de Banda eilanden (1599–1621)*. Batavia: Bataviaasch Genootschap van Kunsten en Wetenschappen.

Churchill, Winston S. (1933–38). *Marlborough: His Life and Times*, 2 vols. London: George G. Harrap & Co.

Cilleßen, Wolfgang (2006). Massaker in der niederländischen Erinnerungskultur: Die Bildwerdung der schwarzen Legende. In Christine Vogel, ed., *Bilder des Schreckens: Die mediale Inszenierung von Massakern seit dem 16. Jahrhundert.* Frankfurt am Main: Campus Verlag.

Colenbrander, Herman Theodoor (1934). *Jan Pietersz. Coen: levenschrijving.* The Hague: Nijhoff.

Dackerman, Susan, Carton, Deborah & The Baltimore Museum of Art (2002). *Painted Prints: The Revelation of Color in Northern Renaissance and Baroque Engravings, Etchings and Woodcuts.* University Park: Pennsylvania State University Press.

Dackerman, Susan, eds. (2011). *Prints and the Pursuit of Knowledge in Early Modern Europe.* Cambridge, MA: Harvard Art Museums.

Daems, James & Nelson, Holly Faith (2019). *Games and War in Early Modern English Literature: From Shakespeare to Swift.* Amsterdam: Amsterdam University Press.

Daudeij, Frank (2021). Romeyn de Hooghe (1645–1708) op de bres voor de burgerlijke eenheid: Het Politiek-Religieuze debat in de Republiek rond 1700 aan de hand van de Spiegel van Staat (1706/07). PhD thesis, Erasmus University Rotterdam.

Davids, Karel (2008). *The Rise and Decline of Dutch Technological Leadership: Technology, Economy and Culture in the Netherlands, 1350– 1800.* Leiden: Brill.

Debord, Guy (1971). *La Société du Spectacle.* Paris: Champ.

De Marchi, Neil & Miegroet, Hans J. van (2006). *Mapping Markets for Paintings in Europe 1450–1750.* Turnhout: Brepols.

Dekker, Rudolf (1979). *Oproeren in Holland gezien door tijdgenoten.* Assen: Van Gorcum.

Dekker, Rudolf (1982). *Holland in beroering: Oproeren in de 17de en 18de eeuw.* Baarn: Ambo.

Deursen, Arie Th. van (1991). *Mensen van klein vermogen: Het kopergeld van de Gouden Eeuw.* Amsterdam: Bert Bakker.

Dijck, José van (2008). Digital Cadavers and Virtual Dissection. In Maaike Bleeker, ed., *Anatomy Live, Performance and the Operating Theatre.* Amsterdam: Amsterdam University Press, pp. 29–48.

Dijkstra, Trude (2018). 'Tot een eeuwige memorie de druckerye-konste': Simon de Vries's Discourse on the Chinese Art of Print 1682. *Quaerendo*, 48 (3), 206–32.

Dijkstra, Trude (2021). *The Chinese Imprint: Printing and Publishing Chinese Religion and Philosophy in the Dutch Republic 1595–1700.* Leiden: Brill.

Domselaer, Tobias van (1665). *Beschryvinge van Amsterdam*, book 4. Amsterdam: Van Doornick.

Duijnen, Michel van (2018). 'Only the Strangest and Most Horrible Cases': The Role of Judicial Violence in the Work of Jan Luyken. *Early Modern Low Countries*, 2 (2), 169–97.

Duijnen, Michel van (2019). A Violent Imagination: Printed Images of Violence in the Dutch Republic 1650–1700. PhD thesis, Vrije Universiteit Amsterdam.

Duijnen, Michel van (2020). From Artless to Artful: Illustrated Histories of the Eighty Years' War in the Seventeenth-Century Dutch Republic. *Low Countries Historical Review*, 135 (2), 4–33.

Duits, Henk (1997). Vondel en de Vrede van Munster: ambivalente gevoelens. *De Zeventiende Eeuw*, 13, 183–90.

Dwyer, Philip & Damousi, Joy, eds. (2020). *The Cambridge World History of Violence, Vol. 3: AD 1500–AD 1800*. Cambridge: Cambridge University Press.

Dwyer, Philip & Micale, Mark, eds. (2021). *The Darker Angels of Our Nature: History, Violence, and the Steven Pinker Controversy*. London: Bloomsbury Academic.

Egmond, Florike (2003). Execution, Pain and Infamy: A Morphological Investigation. In Florike Egmond and Rob Zwijnenberg, eds., *Bodily Extremities: Preoccupations with the Human Body in Early Modern European Culture*. Aldershot: Ashgate, pp. 92–128.

Elenbaas, Rick (2004). De verbouwing van de Amsterdamse Schouwburg (1663–1665) in relatie tot het repertoire, het publiek en de toneelorganisatie. *De Zeventiende Eeuw*, 20, 285–98.

Emmer, Piet (2005). *The Dutch Slave Trade, 1500–1850*. New York: Berghahn.

Emsley, Clive (2007). *Crime, Police and Penal Policy: European Experiences 1750–1940*. Oxford: Oxford University Press.

Erenstein, Rob, ed. (1996). *Een theatergeschiedenis der Nederlanden*. Amsterdam: Amsterdam University Press.

Eversmann, Peter G. F. (2013). 'Founded for the Ears and the Eyes of the People': Picturing the Amsterdam Schouwburg from 1637. In Jan Bloemendal, Peter G. F. Eversman and Elsa Strietman, eds., *Drama, Performance and Debate: Theatre and the Public Opinion in the Early Modern Period*. Leiden: Brill, pp. 269–95.

Fatah-Black, Karwan & Rossum, Matthias van (2016). A Profitable Debate? *Slavery and Abolition: A Journal of Slave and Post-Slave Studies*, 37 (4), 736–43.

Fischer-Lichte, Erika. (2012). *Ästhetik des Performativen*. Frankfurt am Main: Suhrkamp.

Fontaine, Laurence (2014). *The Moral Economy: Poverty Credit and Thrust in Early Modern Europe*. New York: Cambridge University Press.

Frevert, Ute (2011). Gefühle und Kapitalismus. In Gunilla Budde, ed., *Kapitalismus: Historische Annäherungen*. Göttingen: Vandenhoeck & Ruprecht, pp. 50–72.

Friedland, Paul (2012). *Seeing Justice Done: The Age of Spectacular Capital Punishment in France*. Oxford: Oxford University Press.

Frijhoff, Willem (1996). Feesten in de 18de eeuw. In Paul Knolle, ed., *Een groot gedruis en eene onbesuisde vrolykheid. Feesten in de 18e eeuw*. Enschede: Rijksmuseum Twente, pp. 7–30.

Frijhoff, Willem (2016). Fiery Metaphors in the Public Space: Celebratory Culture and Political Consciousness around the Peace of Utrecht. In Renger E. de Bruin, Cornelis van der Haven, Lotte Jensen & David Onnekink, eds., *Performances of Peace: Utrecht 1713*. Leiden: Brill, pp. 223–48.

Frijhoff, Willem & Spies, Marijke (2004). *Dutch Culture in a European Perspective: 1650, Hard-Won Unity*. Assen: Van Gorcum.

Gatens, Moira & Lloyd, Genevieve (1999). *Collective Imaginings: Spinoza, Past and Present*. London: Routledge.

Geerdink, Nina (2012). *De sociale verankering van het dichterschap van Jan Vos (1610–1667)*. Hilversum: Verloren.

Gemert, Lia van (2008). Severing What Was Joined Together: Debates about Pain in the Seventeenth-Century Dutch Republic. In Jan Frans van Dijkhuizen and Karl A. E. Enenkel, eds., *Sense of Suffering: Constructions of Physical Pain in Early Modern Literature*. Leiden: Brill, pp. 443–68.

Goes, Antonides van der (1671). *De Ystroom*. Amsterdam: Pieter Arentsz.

Goldfarb, Hilliard T. (1990). Callot and the Miseries of War: The Artist, His Intentions, and His Context. In Hilliard T. Goldfarb and Reva Wolf, eds., *Fatal Consequences: Callot, Goya, and the Horrors of War*. Hanover: Hood Museum of Art, pp. 13–26.

Goldgar, Anne (2008). *Tulipmania: Money, Honor and Knowledge in the Dutch Golden Age*. Chicago, IL: Chicago University Press.

Gottfried, Johann Ludwig (1698). *Historische kronyck; vervattende een [...] beschrijvingh der aldergedenckwaerdigste geschiedenissen des weerelds, van den aenvangh der scheppingh tot [...] 1576*, 2 vols. Leiden: Pieter van der Aa.

Graeber, David (2001). *Toward an Anthropological Theory of Value: The False Coin of Our Own Dreams*. Basingstoke: Palgrave Macmillan.

Griffiths, Antony (1996). *Prints and Printmaking: An Introduction to the History and Techniques*. London: British Museum.

Groesen, Michiel van (2008). *The Representations of the Overseas World in the De Bry Collection of Voyages (1590–1634)*. Leiden: Brill.

Grootes, Eddy Klaas (1993). Literatuur-recensies 'De Oostersche Schouburgh'. *Literatuur*, 93 (1), 181–2

Haks, Donald (2013). *Vaderland & Vrede 1672–1713: Publiciteit over de Nederlandse Republiek in oorlog*. Hilversum: Verloren.

Hale, Meredith (2007). Political Martyrs and Popular Prints in the Netherlands in 1672: The Murders of Jan and Cornelis de Witt in the Early Modern Media. In Martin Gosman and Joop W. Koopmans, eds., *Selling and Rejecting Politics in Early Modern Europe*. Leuven: Peeters, pp. 119–34.

Hansen, Julie V. (1996). Resurrecting Death: Anatomical Art in the Cabinet of Dr. Frederick Ruysch. *The Art Bulletin*, 78 (4), 663–79.

Haraway, Donna, Ishikawa, Noboru, Scott, Gilbert et al. (2016). Anthropologists Are Talking – About the Anthropocene. *Ethnos*, 81 (3), 535–64.

Harms, Robert W., Blight, David W. & Freamon, Bernard K., eds. (2013). *Indian Ocean Slavery in the Age of Abolition*. New Haven, CT: Yale University Press.

Haven, Cornelis van der (2004). 'Dat heeft men uw Beleid, uw groot Beleid te danken': Theatrale vieringen van de Vrede van Rijswijk (1697) in Amsterdam en Hamburg. *Holland, Historisch Tijdschrift*, 36 (4), 314–26.

Haven, Cornelis van der (2016). Theatres of War and Diplomacy on the Early-Eighteenth-Century Amsterdam Stage. In Renger E. de Bruin, Cornelis van der Haven, Lotte Jensen & David Onnekink, eds., *Performances of Peace: Utrecht 1713*. Leiden: Brill, pp. 181–96.

Haven, Cornelis van der, Korsten, Frans-Willem, Leemans, Inger et al. (2021). Imagineering, or What Images Do to People: Violence and the Spectacular in the Seventeenth-Century Dutch Republic. *Cultural History*, 10 (1), 1–10.

Heckscher, William S. (1958). *Rembrandt's Anatomy of Dr. Tulp*. New York: New York University Press.

Hewitt, Barnard, ed. (1958). *The Renaissance Stage: Documents of Serlio, Sabbattini and Furtenbach*. Coral Gables, FL: University of Miami Press.

Hinterding, Erik, Luijten, Ger & Royalton-Kisch, Martin (2000). *Rembrandt the Printmaker*. Zwolle: Waanders.

Hirschman, Albert O. (1977). *The Passions and the Interests: Political Arguments for Capitalism before Its Triumph*. Princeton, NJ: Princeton University Press.

Hochschild, Arlie Russell (1983). *The Managed Heart: Commercialization of Human Feeling*. Berkeley: University of California.

Hoftijzer, Paul G. (1999). *Pieter van der Aa (1659–1733): Leids drukker en boekverkoper*. Hilversum: Verloren.

Holzhey, Tanja (2014). 'Als gy maar schérp wordt, zo zyn wy, én gy voldaan': Rationalistische ideeën van het kunstgenootschap Nil Volentibus Arduum 1669–1680. PhD thesis, University of Amsterdam.

Hooghe, Romeyn de (1700). *Les Indes Orientales et Occidentales, et autres lieux, représentés en très-belles figures, qui montrent au naturel les peuples, moeurs, religions, fêtes, sacrifices, mosqées, idoles, richesses, ceremonies, festins, tribunaux, supplices et esclavages, comme aussi les montagnes, vaisseaux, commerce, etc.* Leiden: Pieter van der Aa.

Hoorn, Nicolaas ten (1713). *Wegwyzer door Amsterdam.* Amsterdam: Nicolaas ten Hoorn.

Hummelen, Willem M. H. (1967). *Inrichting en gebruik van het toneel in de Amsterdamse Schouwburg van 1637.* Verhandelingen der Koninklijke Nederlandse Akademie van Wetenschappen LXXIII (3). Amsterdam: KNAW.

Hummelen, W. M. H. (1996). Jacob van Campen bouwt de Amsterdamse schouwburg. In Rob L. Erenstein, ed., *Een theatergeschiedenis der Nederlanden.* Amsterdam: Amsterdam University Press, pp. 192–203.

Hunt, Lynn, Jacob, Margaret C. & Mijnhardt, Wijnand (2010). *The Book That Changed Europe: Picart and Bernard's 'Religious Ceremonies of the World'.* Cambridge, MA: Belknap Press of Harvard University Press.

Hutter, Michael (2011). Infinite Surprises: On the Stabilization of Value in the Creative Industries. In Jens Beckert and Patrick Aspers, eds., *The Worth of Goods: Valuation and Pricing in the Economy.* Oxford: Oxford University Press, pp. 201–220.

Illouz, Eva (2007). *Cold Intimacies: The Making of Emotional Capitalism.* Oxford: Wiley.

Israel, Jonathan (1998). *The Dutch Republic: Its Rise, Greatness, and Fall 1477–1806.* Oxford: Clarendon.

Israel, Jonathan (2001). *Radical Enlightenment: Philosophy and the Making of Modernity 1650–1750.* Oxford: Oxford University Press.

Jacob, Margaret C. & Secretan, Catherine, eds. (2008). *The Self-Perception of Early Modern Capitalists.* New York: Palgrave Macmillan.

Jacob, Margaret C. & Secretan, Catherine (2013). Introduction. In Margaret C. Jacob and Catherine Secretan, eds., *In Praise of Ordinary People: Early Modern Britain and the Dutch Republic.* Basingstoke: Palgrave, pp. 1–16.

Jautze, Kim J., Francés, Leonor Álvarez & Blom, Frans (2016). Spaans theater in de Amsterdamse Schouwburg (1638–1672): Kwantitatieve en kwalitatieve analyse van de creatieve industrie van het vertalen. *De Zeventiende Eeuw*, 32, 12–39.

Johannes, Gert-Jan & Leemans, Inger (2018). 'Oh Thou Great God of Trade, O Subject of my Song!' Dutch Poems on Trade, 1770–1830. *Eighteenth Century Studies*, 51 (3), 337–56.

Johannes, Gert-Jan & Leemans, Inger (2020). *De vliegerende Hollander: Cultuurgeschiedenis van de Nederlandse vliegerverbeelding vanaf 1600.* Amsterdam: Prometheus.

Jörg, Christiaan J. A. (1997). *Chinese Ceramics in the Collection of the Rijksmuseum, Amsterdam: The Ming and Qing Dynasties.* London: Philip Wilson.

Knox, Paul & Pinch, Steven (2010). *Urban Social Geography: An Introduction.* London: Routledge.

Kolfin, Elmer & Veen, Jaap van der (2011). *Gedrukt tot Amsterdam: Amsterdamse prentmakers en uitgevers in de Gouden Eeuw.* Zwolle: Waanders.

Kooijmans, Luuc (2004). *De doodskunstenaar: De anatomische lessen van Frederik Ruysch.* Amsterdam: Bert Bakker.

Korsten, Frans-Willem (2017). *A Dutch Republican Baroque: Theatricality, Dramatization, Moment and Event.* Amsterdam: Amsterdam University Press.

Korsten, Frans-Willem & McGourty, Lucy (2023). Babylonian Arrogance in Vondel's "Mars Tamed": A Baroque Allegory Performing Contradiction. *Early Modern Low Countries*, 7 (1).

Korsten, Frans-Willem & Dijk, Marijn van (2020). Violence Heard: The Ekphrasis of Sound from Thundering Sea Battles to Thick Silence. *Journal of the Northern Renaissance*, 11, 433–46.

Kuijpers, Erika (2018). De wonden van een burgeroorlog: Ooggetuigen van het bloed van Naarden in 1572. In Fred van Lieburg, ed., *Geschiedenis aan de Zuidas: Essays van VU-historici.* Amsterdam: Prometheus, pp. 55–63.

Kurtz, Gerdina Hendrika (1928). *Willem III en Amsterdam 1683–1685.* Utrecht: Kemink.

Kuyper, W. (1970). Een maniëristisch theater van een barok architect. *Bulletin van de Koninklijke Nederlandse Oudheidkundige Bond*, 69, 99–117.

Landau, David & Parshall, Peter (1994). *The Renaissance Print, 1470–1550.* New Haven, CT: Yale University Press.

Langbein, John H. (1977). *Torture and the Law of Proof: Europe and England in the Ancien Régime.* Chicago, IL: University of Chicago Press.

Langbein, John H. (1978). Torture and Plea Bargaining. *The University of Chicago Law Review*, 46 (1), 3–22.

Leemans, Inger (2021a). The Amsterdam Stock Exchange As Affective Economy. In Inger Leemans and Anne Goldgar, eds., *Early Modern Knowledge Societies As Affective Economies.* New York: Routledge, pp. 303–30.

Leemans, Inger (2021b). Commercial Desires in a Web of Interest: Dutch Discourses on (Self)-Interest, 1600–1830. In Christine Zabel, ed., *Historicizing Self-Interest in the Modern Atlantic World: A Plea for Ego?* London: Routledge, pp. 141–63.

Leemans, Inger & Goldgar, Anne, eds. (2020). *Early Modern Knowledge Societies as Affective Economies*. London: Routledge.

Leemans, Inger & Johannes, Gert-Jan (2013). *Worm en donder: Geschiedenis van de Nederlandse literatuur 1700–1800*. Amsterdam: Bert Bakker.

Leemans, Inger & Johannes, Gert-Jan (2017). The Kite of State: The Political Iconography of Kiting in the Dutch Republic 1600–1800. *Early Modern Low Countries*, 1 (2), 201–30.

Lehmann, Hauke, Roth, Hans & Schankweiler, Kerstin (2019). Affective Economies. In Jan Slaby and Christian von Scheve, eds., *Affective Societies: Key Concepts*. London: Routledge, pp. 140–51.

Lesger, Clé (2006). *The Rise of the Amsterdam Market and Information Exchange: Merchants, Commercial Expansion and Change in the Spatial Economy of the Low Countries, c.1550–1630*. Florence: Taylor & Francis.

Leuve, Roeland van (1723). *'s Waerelds Koopslot of de Amsteldamse beurs, bestaande in drie Boeken met zeer veele Verbeeldingen*. Amsterdam: J. Verheyden.

Lincoln, Evelyn (2000). *The Invention of the Italian Renaissance Printmaker*. New Haven, CT: Yale University Press.

Loth, Vincent (1995). Pioneers and Perkeniers: The Banda Islands in the 17th Century. *Cakalele*, 6, 13–35.

Loughman, John & Montias, John M. (2000). *Public and Private Spaces: Works of Art in Seventeenth Century Dutch Houses*. Zwolle: Waanders.

Lucassen, Jan. (2004). A Multinational and Its Labor Force: The Dutch East India Company, 1595–1795. *International Labor and Working-Class History*, 66, 12–39.

Margócsy, Dániel (2014). *Commercial Visions: Science, Trade and Visual Culture in the Dutch Golden Age*. Chicago, IL: University of Chicago Press.

Mauss, Marcel (1970). *The Gift: Forms and Functions of Exchange in Archaic Societies*. London: Cohen & West.

McCloskey, Deirdre N. (2006). *The Bourgeois Virtues: Ethics for an Age of Commerce*. Chicago, IL: University of Chicago Press.

McCloskey, Deirdre N. (2016). *Bourgeois Equality: How Ideas, Not Capital or Institutions, Enriched the World*. Chicago, IL: University of Chicago Press.

Mertens, Frank (2012). *Van den Enden en Spinoza*. Amsterdam: Spinozahuis.

Montias, John M. (1982). *Artists and Artisans in Delft: A Socio-Economic Study of the Seventeenth Century*. Princeton, NJ: Princeton University Press.

Montias, John M. (2002). *Art and Auction in Amsterdam in the Seventeenth Century*. Amsterdam: Amsterdam University Press.

Mooij, Annet (1999). *De polsslag van de stad. 350 jaar academische geneeskunde in Amsterdam*. Amsterdam: Arbeiderspers.

Nierop, Henk F. K. van (1999). *Het verraad van het Noorderkwartier: Oorlog, terreur en recht in de Nederlandse Opstand*. Amsterdam: Bakker.

Nierop, Henk F. K. van (2009). *Treason in the Northern Quarter: War, Terror, and the Rule of Law in the Dutch* Revolt, trans. J. C. Grayson. Princeton, NJ: Princeton University Press.

Nierop, Henk F. K. van (2018). *The Life of Romeyn de Hooghe 1645–1708: Prints, Pamphlets, and Politics in the Dutch Golden Age*. Amsterdam: Amsterdam University Press.

Nieuwenhuis, Ivo (2016). Politiek op de kermis: Het genre van de gefingeerde rarekiekvertoning. *Mededelingen van de Stichting Jacob Campo Weyerman*, 39, 1–16.

Nussbaum, Martha (2001). *Upheavals of Thought: The Intelligence of Emotions*. Cambridge: Cambridge University Press.

Nussbaum, Martha (2013). *Political Emotions. Why Love Matters for Justice*. Cambridge, MA: Harvard University Press.

Onnekink, David (2018). The Body Politic. In Helmer Helmers and Geert Janssen, eds., *The Cambridge Companion to the Dutch Golden Age*. Cambridge: Cambridge University Press, pp. 107–23.

Onnekink, David & Rommelse, Gijs (2019). *The Dutch in the Early Modern World: A History of a Global Power*. Cambridge: Cambridge University Press.

Outram, Quentin (2002). The Demographic Impact of Early Modern Warfare. *Social Science History*, 26 (2), 245–72.

Paalvast, Peter (2011). *Martelen en martelwerktuigen in cultuurhistorisch perspectief: De collectie van de Gevangenenpoort nader bekeken*. Zoetermeer: Free Musketeers.

Paepe, Timothy De (2015). Computervisualisaties van de theaterarchitectuur in de Lage Landen (1600–1800). In Thomas Crombez, Jelle Koopmans, Frank Peeters, Luk Van den Dries and Karel Vanhaesebrouck, eds., *Theater: Een Westerse geschiedenis*. Tielt: Lannoo, pp. 145–55.

Park, Katherine & Daston, Lorraine (2016). *The Cambridge History of Science, Vol. 3: Early Modern Science*. Cambridge: Cambridge University Press.

Peat, Rachel (2020). *Japan: Courts and Culture*. London: Royal Collection Trust.

Peters, Edward (1985). *Torture*. New York: B. Blackwell.

Pettegree, Andrew & Der Weduwen, Arthur (2018). What Was Published in the Seventeenth Century Dutch Republic? *Livre: Revue Historique, Société Bibliographique de France*, 1–22.

Pieters, Jürgen (1999). General Introduction. In Jürgen Pieters, ed., *Critical Self-Fashioning: Stephen Greenblatt and the New Historicism*. Frankfurt am Main: Lang, pp. 11–20.

Pieters, Jürgen & Rogiest, Julie (2009). Self-Fashioning in de vroegmoderne literatuur- en cultuurgeschiedenis: genese en ontwikkeling van een concept. *Frame*, 22, 43–59.

Pinker, Steven (2011). *The Better Angels of Our Nature: The Decline of Violence in History and Its Causes*. London: Allen Lane.

Plamper, Jan (2015). *The History of Emotions: An Introduction*. Oxford: Oxford University Press.

Poelwijk, Arjan H. (2003). *'In dienste vant suyckerenbacken': De Amsterdamse suikernijverheid en haar ondernemers, 1580–1630*. Hilversum: Verloren.

Pollmann, Judith (2017). *Memory in Early Modern Europe, 1500–1800*. Oxford: Oxford University Press.

Pollmann, Judith (2018). The Cult and Memory of War and Violence. In Helmer Helmers and Geert Janssen, eds., *The Cambridge Companion to the Dutch Golden Age*. Cambridge: Cambridge University Press, pp. 87–104.

Pomeranz, Kenneth & Topik, Steven (1999). *The World That Trade Created: Society, Culture, and the World Economy, 1400 to the Present*. Armonk, NY: M. E. Sharpe.

Pook, Jan (1709). *Rommelzoodje: Eerste Harlequin, reizende met zijn Rarekiek*. Amsterdam: Timotheus ten Hoorn.

Porta, Antonio (1975). *Joan en Gerrit Corver: De politieke macht van Amsterdam 1702–1748*. Assen: Van Gorcum.

Porteman, Karel & Smits-Veldt, Mieke B. (2008). *Een nieuw vaderland voor de muzen: Geschiedenis van de Nederlandse literatuur 1560–1700*. Amsterdam: Bert Bakker.

Prak, Maarten (2005). *The Dutch Republic in the Seventeenth Century: The Golden Age*. Cambridge: Cambridge University Press.

Protschky, Susie (2011). Between Corporate and Familial Responsibilities: Johan Maurits van Nassau-Siegen and Masculine Governance in Europe and the Dutch Colonial World. In Jacqueline Van Gent and Susan Broomhall, eds., *Governing Masculinities in the Early Modern Period: Regulating Selves and Others*. London: Ashgate, pp. 153–72.

Prud'homme van Reine, Ronald B. (2013). *Moordenaars van Jan de Witt: De zwartste bladzijde van de Gouden Eeuw*. Amsterdam: Arbeiderspers.

Quigley, Christine (2012). *Dissection on Display: Cadavers, Anatomists and Public Spectacle*. Jefferson, NC: McFarland & Company.

Rasterhoff, Claartje (2017). *The Fabric of Creativity in the Dutch Republic: Painting and Publishing As Cultural Industries, 1580–1800*. Amsterdam: Amsterdam University Press.

Rasterhoff, Claartje & Beelen, Kaspar (2020). Coordination in Early Modern Dutch Book Markets: Always Something New. In Inger Leemans and Anne Goldgar, eds., *Early Modern Knowledge Societies As Affective Economies*. London: Routledge, pp. 228–51.

Read, Jason (2015). *The Politics of Transindividuality*. Leiden: Brill.

Reddy, William M. (2001). *The Navigation of Feeling: A Framework for the History of Emotions*. Cambridge: Cambridge University Press.

Reinders, Michel (2010). *Gedrukte Chaos: Populisme en moord in het Rampjaar 1672*. Amsterdam: Balans.

Romein, Jan & Romein-Verschoor, Annie (1977). *Erflaters van onze beschaving*. Amsterdam: Querido.

Rooden, Peter van (1992). Dissenters en bededagen: Civil Religion ten tijde van de Republiek. *Bijdragen en Mededelingen betreffende de Geschiedenis der Nederlanden*, 107 (4), 703–12.

Rossum, van Matthias (2015). *Kleurrijke tragiek: de geschiedenis van Slavernij in Azië onder de VOC*. Hilversum: Verloren.

Rowen, Herbert H. (1978). *Johan de Witt, Grand Pensionary of Holland, 1625–1672*. Princeton, NJ: Princeton University Press.

Rupp, Jan C. C. (1991). Theatra Anatomica: Culturele centra in het Nederland van de zeventiende eeuw. In Joost J. Kloek and Wijnand W. Mijnhardt, eds., *De productie, distributie en consumptie van cultuur*. Amsterdam: Rodopi, pp. 13–36.

Ruysch, Frederik (1744). *Alle de ontleed-genees-en heelkundige werken*, vol. 2. Amsterdam: Janssoons van Waesberge.

Sailer, Richard F. (1957). 'BRAINSTORMING IS IMAGination engINEERING'. *National Carbon Company Management Magazine*.

Salatino, Kevin (1997). *Incendiary Art: The Representation of Fireworks in Early Modern Europe*. Los Angeles, CA: Getty Research Institute.

Sawday, Jonathan (1995). *The Body Emblazoned: Dissection and the Human Body in Renaissance Culture*. London: Routledge.

Schama, Simon (1988). *The Embarrassment of Riches: An Interpretation of Dutch Culture in the Golden Age*. Berkeley: University of California Press.

Scheer, Monique (2012). Are Emotions a Kind of Practice (And What Makes Them Have a History)? A Bourdieuian Approach to Understanding Emotion, *History and Theory*, 51 (2), 193–220.

Schenk, Leon (1670–90). *De droeve Ellendigheden van den Oorloogh: Seer aerdigh en konstigh Afgebeeldt door Iaques Callot. Loreijns Edelman*. Amsterdam: Gerret van Schagen.

Schleifer, Andrei (2000). *Inefficient Markets: An Introduction to Behavioral Finance*. Oxford: Oxford University Press.

Schmidt, Benjamin (2015). *Inventing Exoticism: Geography, Globalism, and Europe's Early Modern World*. Philadelphia: University of Pennsylvania Press.

Siegert, Bernard (2015). *Cultural Techniques: Grids, Filters, Doors and Other Articulations of the Real*, trans. G. Winthrop-Young. New York: Fordham University Press.

Silverman, Lisa (2010). *Tortured Subjects: Pain, Truth, and the Body in Early Modern France*. Chicago, IL: University of Chicago Press.

Sint Nicolaas, Eveline and Valika Smeulders, eds. (2021). *Slavery. An Exhibition of Many Voices*. Amsterdam: Atlas Contact.

Spierenburg, Pieter C. (1984). *The Spectacle of Suffering: Executions and the Evolution of Repression: From a Preindustrial Metropolis to the European Experience*. Cambridge: Cambridge University Press.

Spierenburg, Pieter C. (1991). *The Prison Experience: Disciplinary Institution and Their Inmates in Early Modern Europe*. New Brunswick, NJ: Rutgers University Press.

Spies, Marijke (2001). Amsterdamse doolhoven: Populair cultureel vermaak in de zeventiende eeuw. *Literatuur*, 18, 70–8.

Spinoza, Benedict (1958). *Spinoza: The Political Works*, ed. and trans. A. G. Wernham. Oxford: Clarendon.

Spivak, Gayatri Chakravorty (1988). *Can the Subaltern Speak?* Basingstoke: Macmillan.

Stanziani, Alessandro (2020). Slavery and Post Slavery in the Indian Ocean World. *Hal Open Science*, hal-02556369. https://hal.archives-ouvertes.fr /hal-02556369/document.

Stipriaan, René van (2016). *Lof der botheid: Hoe de Hollanders hun naïviteit verloren*. Amsterdam: Querido.

Storms, Martijn (2011). De kaart van Nederlands Brazilië door Georg Marcgraf. *Caert-thresoor: tijdschrift voor de historische kartografie in Nederland*, 30 (2), 37–46.

Stronks, Els (2011). *Negotiating Differences: Word, Image and Religion in the Dutch Republic*. Leiden: Brill.

Sturkenboom, Dorothee (2019). *De ballen van de Koopman: Mannelijkheid en Nederlandse identiteit in de tijd van de Republiek*. Gorredijk: Sterck & De Vreese.

Suitner, Johannes (2015). *Imagineering Cultural Vienna: On the Semiotic Regulation of Vienna's Culture-Led Urban Transformation*. Bielefeld: Transcript.

Surgers, Anne (2009). *Scénographie du théâtre occidental*. Paris: Armand Colin.

Terjanian, Anoush F. (2013). *Commerce and Its Discontents in Eighteenth-Century French Political Thought*. Cambridge: Cambridge University Press.

Trigg, S. (2016). Affect Theory. In Susan Broomhall, ed., *Early Modern Emotions: An Introduction*. London: Routledge, pp. 10–13.

Turner, Henry S. (2013). *Early Modern Theatricality*. Oxford: Oxford University Press.

Vanhaesebrouck, Karel. (2015). Barok en Classicisme. In Thomas Crombez, Jelle Koopmans, Frank Peeters et al., eds., *Theater: Een westerse geschiedenis*. Tielt: Lanoo, pp. 120–44.

Vega, Lope Félix de (1648). *De beklaagelycke dwang. Bly-eindend Treurspel. In Nederduytsche Rijmen gestelt door Isaak Vos*, 1st ed. Amsterdam: Gillis Joosten for A. K. van Germez.

Vega, Lope Félix de (1671). *De beklaagelycke dwang. Bly-eindend Treurspel. In Nederduytsche Rijmen gestelt door Isaak Vos*, rev. ed. Amsterdam: Jacob Lescailje.

Vondel, Joost van den (1655). *Inwydinge van 't Stadthuis t'Amsterdam*. Amsterdam: T. Fontein for wed. A. de Wees.

Vondel, Joost van den (1929). Voorspel. In Johannes F. M. Sterck, H. W. E. Moller, C. G. N. de Voys et al., eds., *De werken van Vondel: Derde deel 1663–1674*. Amsterdam: De Maatschappij voor goede en goedkoope lectuur, pp. 523–5.

Vondel, Joost van den (1931). De getemde Mars. In Johannes F. M. Sterck, H. W. E. Moller, C. G. N. de Voys et al., eds., *De werken van Vondel: Vijfde deel 1645–1656*. Amsterdam: De Maatschappij voor goede en goedkoope lectuur, pp. 250–7.

Vondel, Joost van den (1935). Zeemagazyn. In Johannes F. M. Sterck, H. W. E. Moller, C. G. N. de Voys et al., eds., *De werken van Vondel: Achtste deel 1656–1660*. Amsterdam: De Maatschappij voor goede en goedkoope lectuur, pp. 653–65.

Vondel, Joost van den (1937). Zegezang over den zeestrijt der doorluchtighste heren staeten, door den weledelen en gestrengen Michaël Ruyter. In Johannes F. M. Sterck, H. W. E. Moller, C. G. N. de Voys et al., eds., *De werken van Vondel: Tiende deel 1663–1674*. Amsterdam: De Maatschappij voor goede en goedkoope lectuur, pp. 209–13.

Vos, Jan (1667). *Medea*. Amsterdam: Jacob Lescailje.

Vos, Jan (1671). *Medea*. In Jan Vos, *Alle de gedichten van den vermaarden Poëet Jan Vos*, vol. 2. Amsterdam: Jacob Lescailje.

Vos, Jan (1699). *Aran en Titus of wraek en weerwraek*, 17th ed. Amsterdam: Wed. Gijsbert de Groot.

Vos, Jan (1975). Aan de beminnaars van d'oude en nieuwe toneelspeelen. In Jan Vos, *Toneelwerken*, ed. W. J. C. Buitendijk. Assen: Van Gorcum, p. 353.

Vries, Jan de & Woude, Ad M. van der (1997). *The First Modern Economy: Success, Failure, and Perseverance of the Dutch Economy, 1500–1815*. Cambridge: Cambridge University Press.

Wagener, Hans-Jürgen (1994). Cupiditate et Potentia: The Political Economy of Spinoza. *The European Journal of the History of Economic Thought*, 1 (3), 475–93.

Wallerstein, Immanuel ([1980] 2011). *The Modern World-System, Vol. 2: Mercantilism and the Consolidation of the European World Economy: 1600–1750*. Berkeley: University of California Press.

Weststeijn, Arthur (2012). *Commercial Republicanism in the Dutch Golden Age: The Political Thought of Johan and Pieter de la Court*. Leiden: Brill.

Widjojo, Muridan Satrio (2009). *The Revolt of Prince Nuku: Cross-Cultural Alliance-Making in Maluku, c.1780–1810*. Leiden: Brill.

Yazdipour, Rassoul (2011). *Advances in Entrepreneurial Finance*. New York: Springer.

Zanden, Jan Luiten van (2009). *The Long Road to the Industrial Revolution: The European Economy in a Global Perspective, 1000–1800*. Leiden: Brill.

Acknowledgements

This Element is one of the outcomes of a research project entitled 'Imagineering Violence: Techniques of Early Modern Performativity in the Northern and Southern Netherlands (1630–1690)' (ITEMP-Violence), funded by the Research Foundation Flanders (FWO) and the Dutch Research Council (NWO). The research project is a collaboration between Vrije Universiteit Amsterdam, Université libre de Bruxelles, Ghent University and Leiden University. The research group behind it consisted of Yannice de Bruyn, Michel van Duijnen and the authors of this Element. We would like to sincerely thank Michel and Yannice for contributing to the brainwork that went into this Element during the numerous conversations and encounters that took place during the project (2015–19). Their respective PhD theses played a prominent role in the development of the ideas central to this Element. Both Inger Leemans and Karel Vanhaesebrouck received support from the Netherlands Institute for Advanced Studies (NIAS) within the framework of the Global Knowledge Society project to develop their ideas on affective economies. We are grateful to the following colleagues for giving advice on earlier versions of sections and for their suggestions for literature: Geertje Mak, Marrigje Paijmans, Marijn van Dijk, Lucy McGourty, Han van der Vegt and Jan van Dijkhuizen. Our thanks also go to Sophie van den Bergh, who took care of putting together the references, and Kate Delaney and Jon Stacey, for copy-editing the Element. For making this publication available in Open Access, we received generous grants from the Leiden University Centre for the Arts in Society and NL-Lab – KNAW Humanities Cluster. Minor parts of Sections 1 and 5 are based on earlier articles, with kind permission of the concerned publishers: Cornelis van der Haven, Frans-Willem Korsten, Inger Leemans, Karel Vanhaesebrouck, Michel van Duijnen and Yannice De Bruyn, 'Imagineering, or What Images Do to People: Violence and the Spectacular in the Seventeenth-Century Dutch Republic', *Cultural History* 10.1 (2021), 1–10; Inger Leemans and Gert-Jan Johannes, 'The Kite of State: The Political Iconography of Kiting in the Dutch Republic 1600–1800', *Early Modern Low Countries* 1.2 (2017), 201–30; Frans-Willem Korsten and Lucy McGourty, 'Babylonian Arrogance in Vondel's "Mars Tamed": A Baroque Allegory Performing Contradiction', *Early Modern Low Countries* 7.1 (2023).

Cambridge Elements ≡

Histories of Emotions and the Senses

Series Editors

Rob Boddice
Tampere University

Rob Boddice (PhD, FRHistS) is Senior Research Fellow at the Academy of Finland Centre of Excellence in the History of Experiences. He is the author/editor of 13 books, including *Knowing Pain: A History of Sensation, Emotion and Experience* (Polity Press, 2023), *Humane Professions: The Defence of Experimental Medicine, 1876–1914* (Cambridge University Press, 2021) and *A History of Feelings* (Reaktion, 2019).

Piroska Nagy
Université du Québec à Montréal (UQAM)

Piroska Nagy is Professor of Medieval History at the Université du Québec à Montréal (UQAM) and initiated the first research program in French on the history of emotions. She is the author or editor of 14 volumes, including *Le Don des larmes au Moyen Âge* (Albin Michel, 2000); *Medieval Sensibilities: A History of Emotions in the Middle Ages*, with Damien Boquet (Polity, 2018); and *Histoire des émotions collectives: Épistémologie, émergences, expériences*, with D. Boquet and L. Zanetti Domingues (Classiques Garnier, 2022).

Mark Smith
University of South Carolina

Mark Smith (PhD, FRHistS) is Carolina Distinguished Professor of History and Director of the Institute for Southern Studies at the University of South Carolina. He is author or editor of over a dozen books and his work has been translated into Chinese, Korean, Danish, German, and Spanish. He has lectured in Europe, throughout the United States, Australia, and China and his work has been featured in the *New York Times*, the *London Times*, the *Washington Post*, and the *Wall Street Journal*. He serves on the US Commission for Civil Rights.

About the Series

Born of the emotional and sensory "turns," Elements in Histories of Emotions and the Senses move one of the fastest-growing interdisciplinary fields forward. The series is aimed at scholars across the humanities, social sciences, and life sciences, embracing insights from a diverse range of disciplines, from neuroscience to art history and economics. Chronologically and regionally broad, encompassing global, transnational, and deep history, it concerns such topics as affect theory, intersensoriality, embodiment, human-animal relations, and distributed cognition. The founding editor of the series was Jan Plamper.

Cambridge Elements ☰

Histories of Emotions and the Senses

Elements in the Series

Scholastic Affect: Gender, Maternity and the History of Emotions
Clare Monagle

Emotion, Sense, Experience
Rob Boddice and Mark Smith

Playful Virtual Violence: An Ethnography of Emotional Practices in Video Games
Christoph Bareither

Phantom Pains and Prosthetic Narratives: From George Dedlow to Dante
Alastair Minnis

Emotions and Temporalities
Margrit Pernau

Feeling Terrified?: The Emotions of Online Violent Extremism
Lise Waldek, Julian Droogan and Catharine Lumby

Making Noise in the Modern Hospital
Victoria Bates

Academic Emotions: Feeling the Institution
Katie Barclay

Sensory Perception, History and Geology
Richard Read

Love in Contemporary Technoculture
Ania Malinowska

Memes, History and Emotional Life
Katie Barclay and Leanne Downing

Marketing Violence: The Affective Economy of Violent Imageries in the Dutch Republic
Frans-Willem Korsten, Inger Leemans, Cornelis van der Haven and Karel Vanhaesebrouck

A full series listing is available at: www.cambridge.org/EHES

Printed in the United States
by Baker & Taylor Publisher Services